LITTLE GIANT® ENCYCLOPEDIA

TOASTS & QUOTES

LITTLE GIANT® ENCYCLOPEDIA

TOASTS & QUOTES

THE DIAGRAM GROUP

STERLING INNOVATION
An imprint of Sterling Publishing Co., Inc.

New York / London
www.sterlingpublishing.com

Compiled by Jane Johnson, Richard Hummerstone, and Bruce Robertson

To make the compilation consistent the authors have frequently used male pronouns. This is not to infer all comments refer to males. The text can easily be adapted to comments on both men and women.

Library of Congress Cataloging-in-Publication Data

10 9 8 7 6 5 4 3 2 1

Published by Sterling Publishing Company, Inc.
387 Park Avenue South, New York, N.Y. 10016
A Diagram Book first created by Diagram Visual Information Limited of Kentish Town Road, London, England NW5 2JU
© 1998, 2009 by Diagram Visual Information Limited
Distributed in Canada by Sterling Publishing
c/o Canadian Manda Group, 165 Dufferin Street
Toronto, Ontario, Canada M6K 3H6
Distributed in the United Kingdom by GMC Distribution Services
Castle Place, 166 High Street, Lewes, East Sussex, England BN7 1XU
Distributed in Australia by Capricorn Link (Australia) Pty Ltd.
P.O. Box 704, Windsor, NSW 2756, Australia

Printed in China
All rights reserved

Sterling ISBN 978-1-4027-6732-6

For information about custom editions, special sales, premium and corporate purchases, please contact Sterling Special Sales Department at 800-805-5489 or specialsales@sterlingpublishing.com.

Foreword

Have you ever been stuck for words? No ideas to fill out a speech or reply to a friend? *The Little Giant Encyclopedia of Toasts and Quotes* provides you with the answers, together with hints on public speaking.

This invaluable book contains over two thousand witty and wise sentences which will enable you to be bright and intelligent in conversation and correspondence. For ease of access, the quotations, toasts, roasts and proverbs have been grouped under topics. Should you need further quotations from an author, there is an author index.

When using the book, begin with the topic you have in mind. Then browse and select similar topics. You must feel free to adapt the quotes, personalize the ideas for your own needs, and always remember the best effect is achieved by keeping the punch line to the end.

Oscar Wilde, the 19th-century playwright, was dazzling a group of friends at dinner with his wit and wisdom. James McNeill Whistler, the artist, was attending and glumly said of one of Wilde's remarks, *"I wish I had said that."* Wilde replied, *"You will, James, you will."*

Contents

CONTENTS

Public speaking

There are many occasions when you may be called upon to speak in public. Among your family and friends you may speak at gatherings for the birth of a new baby, the graduation of a young person, the marriage of a relative, a birthday or anniversary, a reunion, or a social gathering with friends or club members.

If you are willing, you may have to talk in public about events in your professional life — the introduction of new work members, an introduction of yourself, a person's promotion, or a retirement.

Remember the most important part of your speech is the preparation — the work you put in before you begin to talk. This consists of forming a theme to your speech, doing research on the subject or the person, and embellishing it with quotes and toasts.

If you are making a formal speech, consult a book or an experienced person for information on whom you should toast and thank.

Begin with a note pad and jot down your basic ideas in any order. If you have very few then ask others for ideas. Do research on your subjects — their private lives, company history, or background so you include personal elements in your speech. Consult *The Little Giant Encyclopedia of Toasts and Quotes* for ideas you can include and then use the quotations for support.

Again, collect the material in any order.

Assemble your ideas in note form and check they cover all the necessary points required on the occasion.

When your research is complete and you have lots of good ideas and ingredients, take a new sheet of paper and set out a basic plan for your speech. Build an introduction, a main theme, and an end.

Your speech must have five major elements:

STRUCTURE is based on what you want to say and the order you want to say it in.

SIMPLICITY is avoiding complex ideas and unfamiliar words.

CLARITY is how you express the ideas.

RELEVANCE means understanding your audience and the subject they are waiting for you to explain.

HUMOR comes from your personal memories or your research into source books of jokes.

Cross off all the notes as you place them in the right section. It's easy to take photocopies of your notes and then cut up the stats in the new order — or cut up your notes into strips and arrange them on sheets, checking they are all there before sticking them up.

Once you have your speech in order, carefully copy it all out onto new sheets. This may seem a very wasteful way to create your speech, but each time you re-read or rewrite you build up the ideas in your mind.

Read it all through once and check how long it takes. If it's longer than the time allocated, see if you can combine some ideas. If it's shorter, consult *LGE* for more quotes and ask your friends for more ideas.

Then, read your final notes through again. The purpose of constantly re-reading your speech is to commit it to memory.

Using the full speech, write out each idea in very brief form — as if you were sending a cable or had to pay for every word in a personal ad. These become your notes for the speech when you go up in front of your audience.

Remember your speech must have a beginning, a middle, and an end. This may seem obvious but many people wander about the subject and lose their audience's attention.

Members of the audience look to you to hold their attention so your speech should involve them. Begin by acknowledging them and by praising and thanking them for attending. Getting them on your side makes your talk go smoothly.

Practice the speech before you go, and be sure you remember the main topics. Time yourself to establish the duration of your speech. Remember there will be responses to your statements. Pause if the audience laughs, then continue with the stories.

Using your brief notes, read them out loud, fleshing out the stories to their original length, and again, check how long your speech is.

Many speakers begin their talk with an apology for their inabilities. This builds a sympathy from the audience and at the end of your speech the audience feels you did a good job.

Finally, thank everyone for having listened to you.

Remember, public speaking is very easy — that's why politicians do it all the time — but building a good, well structured, amusing and to the point speech is ninety-eight percent of the task.

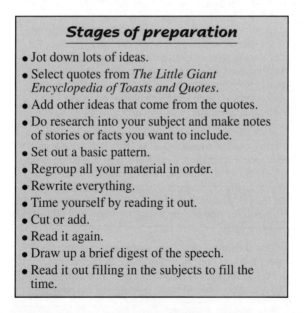

Stages of preparation

- Jot down lots of ideas.
- Select quotes from *The Little Giant Encyclopedia of Toasts and Quotes*.
- Add other ideas that come from the quotes.
- Do research into your subject and make notes of stories or facts you want to include.
- Set out a basic pattern.
- Regroup all your material in order.
- Rewrite everything.
- Time yourself by reading it out.
- Cut or add.
- Read it again.
- Draw up a brief digest of the speech.
- Read it out filling in the subjects to fill the time.

Using quotes

The Little Giant Encyclopedia of Toast and Quotes
provides you with a resource of ideas and humorous
sayings which you can adapt to your own needs. You
can select from different categories — a pick-and-mix
approach. You can modify to suit your audience; and
you can build into your own text ideas derived from the
quotations.

You can choose quotations from the different categories
which are relevant to your subject. For a talk at a
graduation dinner you could take from the Ability and
Achievement section "God will not look you over for
medals, degrees, or diplomas, but for scars!"; from
Appearance,"The expression you wear on your face is
more important than the clothes you wear on your
back." From Crime and Punishment, "You are
remembered for the rules you break."

You can modify the quotation so that it specifically
refers to one of the guests. It is far better to have an
appropriate quotation, even if it's bent a little, than one
which most listeners find obscure and irrelevant. For
example, the biblical quotation "Blessed are the weak
for they shall inherit the earth" was transformed by a
wit into "Blessed are the young for they shall inherit the
national debt."

Within the quotation "They say travel broadens the
mind, but you must have the mind" in the section
Travel, is the idea that you benefit from travel — if you
go in search of knowledge. Within your talk at a

graduation dinner you can express the idea first, then follow up with confirmation by the quote.

Avoid quotations whose meaning is obscure because they are taken out of context. William Wordsworth, a 19th-century British poet is quoted as saying, "The child is the father of the man," but taken out of his poem the line has no immediate clear meaning.

When you include a quote it's often simplest to say, as the American poet Robert Frost once said, "Happiness makes up in height for what it lacks in length." It can also be more comfortable in your speech simply to include the quote as part of your theme and not acknowledge the author. There may be many in the audience who don't recognize the author and feel inadequate because you are more well informed than they are. It's important you don't make your audience uncomfortable.

You can personalize the quote simply by substituting the name of a person. The English dramatist Oscar Wilde said: "I hope you have not been leading a double life, pretending to be wicked and being good all the time." In your speech you could incorporate the idea as "Our guest of honor, Henry, has lead a double life pretending to all of us he's wicked — while all the time he's a good guy."

Deliver your quotes as the punch line of an idea to bring out the point in a sharp, concise, and often humorous way.

Order of speakers at a wedding

Suggested contents of the father's speech:

- His happiness on bringing up his daughter.
- One or two stories, possibly funny, to illustrate the sort of person she is.
- His daughter beginning her new life.
- A welcome to his son-in-law and his parents as new members of the family.
- An item of advice on the couple's future together.

Suggested contents of the groom's speech:

- Thanks to the bride's parents and the bridesmaids.
- Thanks to his parents.
- An amusing story about meeting his bride or their preparations for the wedding.
- Thanks to the ushers and the best man.
- Thanks to the guests for attending.

Suggested contents of the best man's speech:

- Thanks to the groom on behalf of the bridesmaids.
- Anecdotes about the groom.
- Toast to the bride and groom's future happiness.

My speech

- **❝** It usually takes me more than three weeks to prepare a good impromptu speech.
- **❝** I do not object to people looking at their watches when I am speaking. But I strongly object when they start shaking them to make certain they are still going.
- **❝** I may rise without a friend; I hope I can sit down without an enemy.
- **❝** My speech will be like a lady's dress — long enough to cover the subject, and short enough to be interesting.
- **❝** I am a person who is too nervous to eat their meal, who is too unfamiliar with the subject I'm talking about, who has forgotten the punch lines of jokes most of you have already heard.
- **❝** I try to remember that speeches cannot be made long enough for speakers nor short enough for listeners.
- **❝** I fear my speech may be like the fan held by a fan dancer — it will call attention to the subject without making any particular effort to cover it.

♦

Well, we all have one thing in common:
none of us knows what I'm going to say.

Do

- Be prepared, make notes, plan your talk, memorize the quotes.
- Use the quotes to suit the situation.
- Modify the quotes to include relevant details in your speech.
- When you use a quote, be sure the reason for its inclusion is clear to the audience.
- Try to get your audience on your side.
- Keep the jokes and stories suitable for all the audience.
- Keep to the point.
- End on a positive note.

Don't

- Don't use quotes of authors just to show how well read you are.
- Don't use quotes the audience will not understand.
- Don't ever leave the audience with a doubt as to why you included that particular quote.
- Don't ever ad-lib unless you have a good memory and experience.
- Don't wander around your subject.
- Don't disappoint your audience.
- Don't deliberately antagonize the audience.
- Don't be rude, obscene, or say anything that can make people uncomfortable.

At the end of your speech

Should you feel you wish to end your speech with a poem, here are three examples to choose from.

♦

*And the night shall be filled with music,
And the cares that infest the day
Shall fold their tents, like the Arabs,
And as silently steal away.*

♦

*I feel like one
Who treads alone
Some banquet-hall deserted,
Whose lights are fled,
Whose garlands dead,
And all but he departed.*

♦

*I hear a voice you cannot hear,
Which says I must not stay;
I see a hand you cannot see,
Which beckons me away.*

Toasts
and roasts

Toasts & Roasts

When giving a toast make sure that all the guests have a drink in their hand before you announce the toast. It is best to have them prepare for the toast prior to your speech.

Always make the toast a positive and joyful one. Everyone should be wishing the recipient of the toast well.

Name the person or persons after raising your glass and saying a brief toast.

At a marriage you could say: "Let us toast our happy couple, *a marriage made in heaven and lived on earth* — to Joan and Jim."

A toast to marriage

- Made in heaven, lived on earth.
- The triumph of hope over experience.
- A word which, if some people are to be believed, should be pronounced mirage.
- That sacred partnership, the oldest partnership in the world, the most intimate, and the most enduring.
- Marry carefully and love will surely follow.
- Marrying is easy — housekeeping is harder.
- Now you're married we wish you joy. First a girl and then a boy.

66 If necessary, sleep in separate rooms, dine apart, take separate vacations, have different friends. Do everything possible to keep your marriage together.

66 You may both think marriage is a fifty-fifty proposition. If you do — you both don't understand women or percentages.

66 Let it never be said of them they gave each other something to live for — a divorce.

66 When they bought the marriage license he knew it was forever — and threw away the receipt.

To the Bride and Groom
And on her lover's arm she leant,
And round her waist she felt it fold,
And far across the hills they went
In that new world which is the old.

The Groom to his Bride
Drink — Drink to me only with thine eyes,
And I will pledge with mine;
Or leave a kiss but in the cup,
And I'll not look for wine.

To the unmarried at a wedding
Cuckoos lead Bohemian lives,
They fail as husbands and as wives,
And so they cynically disparage
Everybody else's marriage.

At wedding anniversaries

- After so many years of marriage don't believe you are like wine, that you get better with age. If you do, you may end up in the cellar.
- Their marriage seems to have lasted forever — and at times I bet they thought so.
- Their marriage has been forever — with no time off for good behavior.
- Their happiness is due to her ability to think like a man, act like a lady, look like a girl, and work like a slave.
- The groom was very unlucky — he promised his wife everything she could want when a man walked on the moon.
- He's forgotten which day he was married on so has to give his wife gifts whenever she reminds him.

♦

It's nice to see a couple who have been married so long, they must be doing something right — or maybe something wrong.

♦

*The kindest and the happiest pair
Will find occasion to forbear;
And something every day they live
To pity, and perhaps forgive.*

A toast to love

66 The meeting of two persons is like the contact of two chemical substances: if there is a reaction, both are transformed.

66 Those who love you deserve you to love them.

66 Love is blind, friendship closes its eyes.

66 An ounce of love is worth a pound of knowledge.

66 Those of us who have courage to love will need the courage to suffer.

66 In love, as in other worthwhile pastimes, the amateur status must be maintained.

66 Love is real enough — but it has a deadly enemy — and that is life.

◆

I hold it true, whate'er befall;
I feel it, when I sorrow most;
'Tis better to have loved and lost
Than never to have loved at all

◆

Love seeketh not itself to please,
Nor for itself hath any care;
But for another gives its ease,
And builds a heaven in hell's despair

◆

Had we never loved so blindly
Had we never loved so kindly
Never met — or never parted
We would not be now so broken hearted

A toast to graduation

❝ Blessed are the young — for they shall inherit the national debt.

❝ It takes a long time, and a great deal of experience, to be young.

❝ Those the Gods love die young, even if they live to old age.

❝ When you are young you can remember everything, even if it didn't happen.

❝ You are better to waste your youth than to do nothing at all with it.

❝ Your prime is elusive — as you grow older you must be on the alert to recognize it when it occurs.

❝ If you come to your parents for advice, remember they raised you and look where you are now.

♦

It was a rule of Leonardo da Vinci's
Not to put his trust in princes.
Pleading was of no avail;
They had to pay up on the nail.

♦

If you can fill the unforgiving minute
With sixty seconds' worth of distance run
Yours is the earth and everything that's in it,
And — which is more — you'll be a man, my son.

To good friends

❝ Each time you gain one, you become one.

❝ We are counted rich by their number.

❝ It's easier to forgive our enemies' crimes than to forget our friends' faults.

❝ Who, when we are rich, well, and happy, visit us only when asked; but when we are in adversity come without invitation.

❝ A single spirit inhabiting two bodies.

❝ Those who double our joy and halve our sorrows.

❝ Who we must praise in public and criticize only in private.

❝ Who we judge not by their number but by their steadfastness and support.

❝ Those who love us and know our faults and who love us despite our achievements.

❝ When we are a friend to others we are a friend to ourselves.

❝ Who see us at our worst — and still love us.

❝ We may deserve our enemies but we don't deserve our friends.

❝ We are taught to forgive our enemies — but can we forgive our friends?

❝ We get by with a little help from our friends.

❝ It's not their help that supports us, but the knowledge it is there if we need it.

To drink

- ❝ To the man who invented whisky and the man who ate the first oyster.
- ❝ Let's drink a cup of kindness yet, for the sake of old lang syne.
- ❝ While you live, drink! — for, once dead, you never shall return.
- ❝ Drink, for there is no drinking after death.
- ❝ Drink! for you know not whence you came, nor why: Drink! for you know not why you go, nor where.
- ❝ Drinking makes you feel as you ought to feel without drink.
- ❝ Candy is dandy but liquor is quicker.
- ❝ For we may have a drinking problem — it's usually there's never enough.
- ❝ Another little drink won't do us any harm.
- ❝ There are more old drunkards than old physicians.

♦

Fill the glasses fair!
Every drop we sprinkle
O'er the brow of care
Smoothes away a wrinkle

♦

I was leaning against the ceiling
as I walked across the wall
I thought, if the ceiling gives way
I am in for a nasty fall.

♦

Then trust me, there's nothing like drinking
So pleasant on this side of the grave
It keeps the unhappy from thinking
And makes all the rest the more brave

♦

A glass is good, and a lass is good,
And a pipe to smoke in cold weathers,
The world is good, and the people are good,
And we're all good fellows together.

♦

My lips, on your own may print farewell
They never have been soiled by the "beverage of hell"
But they come to you now with a boozy sign
These lips that touched liquor can now touch thine.

♦

What fury of late has crept into our feasts?
What honor is given to we drunken beasts?
What's reputation to bear one glass more?
When we are most likely carried out of the door.

♦

So nigh is grandeur to our dust
So near is drink to man
When duty whispers low,
You must,
We all reply, we can.

♦

When offered drink they sometimes sigh
Theirs is not to stand and reply
Theirs is not to reason why
Theirs is but to drink and die.

A toast to my retirement

❝ I decided to stop working here — that was many years ago. I've enjoyed those times so much I'm going to not work somewhere else.

❝ I stopped working for the company many years ago — I'm just making it official by my retirement.

◆

Remember when you have nothing to do,
there's no one does it better than you.

◆

Too late I stayed — forgive the crime,
Unheeded flew the hours.
How noiseless falls the foot of time,
That only treads on flowers!

◆

I have eaten your bread and salt,
I have drunk your water and wine,
The deaths ye died I have watched beside,
And the lives that ye led were mine.

◆

I will sit beside my lonely fire,
And pray for wisdom yet:
For calmness to remember,
Or courage to forget.

◆

But if upon the troubled sea
Thou hast thrown a gem unheeded,
Hope not that wind or wave will bring
The treasures back when needed.

A toast to a retiring person

66 You can sum up his success here in one word —
   LUCKY.
66 A wise Roman once said "Cessation of work is
   not accompanied by cessation of expenses."
66 You have to put off being young until you can
   retire.

◆

When you're home and thinking what to do,
remember all of us at work are thinking that, too.

◆

His back against a rock he bore,
And firmly placed his foot before:
"Come one, come all, this rock shall fly
From its firm base as soon as I."

◆

Not to the swift, the race:
Not to the strong, the fight:
Not to the righteous, perfect grace:
Not to the wise, the light.

But often faltering feet
Come surest to the goal;
And they who walk in darkness meet
The sunrise of the soul.

◆

Happy the man, and happy he alone,
He who can call today his own:
He who, secure within, can say,
Tomorrow do thy worst, for I have lived today.

Jokes at a wedding

If you tell jokes that could make some people in the room uncomfortable — apologise by saying it's not true.

66 He's had many wives — two of them his own.

66 He's so mean he stores all the gifts he receives along with their labels and at a later date gives them to other friends.

66 She called her accountant one day and said: "Wouldn't it save taxes if I earned less money?"

66 Marriage is like a birdcage in the garden: those inside soon want to get outside and those outside think it's easier inside.

66 He chose his wife just as she did her wedding gown — it looks good and it will wear well.

66 Their marriage will have successful sex. They have the maximum of temptation with the maximum of opportunity.

66 Their marriage will be like a pair or scissors — joined so they cannot be separated. Each moving in different directions — yet dangerous for any one who comes between them.

66 Marriage is a great institution, let's hope neither ends up there.

Jokes at retirement parties

If you tell jokes that could make the person you are addressing feel uncomfortable — add compliments afterwards.

" He worked here on the principle that he put off today what he could do tomorrow. He put off tomorrow what could be done the day after tomorrow — he leaves us with his legacy of undone tasks.

" He carried a rabbit's foot for luck — to remind him how lucky the rabbit was to lose only one leg.

" He would always listen to our troubles. Why not, he caused most of them.

" He's so old that when he orders a three-minute egg, they ask for the money up front.

" He's lived a long life and still doesn't use glasses — he drinks straight out of the bottle.

" Now he's old he can do things he has been dying to do for years — act like a kid.

" He was once asked: "How long have you worked here?" He replied: "About a third of the time I've been here."

♦

What can I tell you about him
He's just a terrific guy
I cannot remember his good points
But his wife asked me to try.

Short poems for all occasions

I eat my peas with honey
I've done it all my life
It makes the peas taste funny
But it keeps 'em on the knife!

♦

The little mice ask how the cheese got there,
And warmly debate the matter;
The Orthodox said it came from the air,
And the Heretics said from the platter.

♦

The drunkard now reclining snores
His load of ale sweats through his pores
Yet when he wakes the drunk shall find,
A headache will remain behind.

♦

You've never had a piece of toast
Sometimes long or sometimes wide
That fell upon a covered floor
And always on the buttered side.

♦

As I was sitting in this chair
I knew the bottom wasn't there,
Nor legs, or back, but I just sat,
Ignoring little things like that.

♦

Here's to the happiest days of my life,
Spent in the arms of another man's wife
— my mother!

♦

Heavenly Father bless us,
And keep us all alive
There's lots of us to dinner
But only booze for five.

♦

The optimist, who always was a fool,
Cries "Look! My mug of ale is still half full."
His brother gives the facts their proper twist —
"My mug's half empty!" sighs the pessimist.

♦

Some of the hurts you have cured,
And the sharpest you still have survived,
But what torments of grief you endured
From evils which never arrived!

♦

There are several reasons for drinking,
And one has just entered my head;
If a man cannot drink when he's living
How the hell can he drink when he's dead?

♦

Nothing to do but work!
Nothing! Alas, alack!
Nowhere to go but out!
Nowhere to come but back!

♦

We may have many faults
But _ _ _ _ _ _ _ _ _ _ has only two
Everything he say
And everything he do.

Roasts for all occasions

" _ _ _ _ _ might as well laugh at himself once in a while — everyone else does.

" _ _ _ _ _ has to learn like every bride that her wedding is not her own — it's her mother's.

" When I asked _ _ _ _ was she a friend of the groom, she said: "Certainly not, I'm the bride's mother."

" I'll never forget my wedding, you never saw such a happy couple — her mother and father.

" _ _ _ _ _ asked me if I thought him vain. "No," I replied, "Why do you ask?" "Well, people as clever as me usually are."

" _ _ _ _ _ wanted to stay on in this job — but officially he's leaving because of illness and fatigue. The boss is sick and tired of him.

" _ _ _ _ _ is a humble and modest man, and with good reason.

" _ _ _ _ _ would have been a movie star — he does the work of two men: Laurel and Hardy.

" _ _ _ _ _ is very diplomatic, he'll talk down to anyone.

" _ _ _ _ _ in anger once gave me a piece of his mind and I was surprized how small it was.

" Today I learnt about spelling. The accent is on the young — but the stress is on the parent.

" My wife learnt a serious lesson today — never lend your car to anyone you have given birth to.

" _ _ _ _ _ once said to me: "When I want your opinion, I'll give it to you."

" _ _ _ _ _ has ruined his health by constantly drinking to everyone else's.

" _ _ _ _ _ will be drunk when he starts acting sophisticated but cannot pronounce it.

" _ _ _ _ _ joined this party as fit as a fiddle, he'll go home as tight as a drum.

" _ _ _ _ _ is the toast of this party, that is why everyone is buttering him up.

" _ _ _ _ _ at our wedding my wife was very jealous — she had male bridesmaids.

" _ _ _ _ _ was asked once: "Why do you always answer a question with a question?" He replied: "Well, why not?"

" My wife thinks I'm like a fire — I go out if unattended.

" Hard work never killed anyone — but why should we take the chance?

" _ _ _ _ _ is very diplomatic, he frequently does what he said he wouldn't.

" _ _ _ _ _ has more talent in his little finger than he has in his whole head.

" I want you to say of me I bring happiness wherever I go — and not whenever I go.

" _ _ _ _ _ has antique furniture in his house — it wasn't antique when he bought it.

" _ _ _ _ _ has always been a good friend, we both dislike the same people.

" _ _ _ _ _ has many acquaintances, that's people he knows well enough to borrow from — but not well enough to lend to.

" _ _ _ _ _ is the sort of friend who's always there when he needs you.

" _ _ _ _ _ has strong views — I tried to tell him an idea is not responsible for the people who believe in it.

" _ _ _ _ _ is like a weed, a plant whose virtues have not yet been discovered.

" _ _ _ _ _ is retiring — but I explained, we are not so much losing a good worker as gaining another parking space.

" _ _ _ _ _ has been looking forward to his retirement but not as much as we have.

" _ _ _ _ _ met his wife at a dance — she was the prettiest thing on the floor. I still remember her lying there.

" _ _ _ _ _ is a perfect gentleman. On the subway he always offers his seat to a lady as he's leaving.

" The young ladies this evening cannot keep their hands off me — they want to prevent me speaking.

" _ _ _ _ _ is living proof that having a goal and struggling hard to attain it doesn't always work.

" _ _ _ _ _ never forgets a kind deed, especially if it is one of his.

" _ _ _ _ _ is now in a position to say anything he wants, as hardly anyone will listen to him.

" _ _ _ _ _ plans to sit on a beach chair and just do nothing — that way he feels like he's back at the office.

" _ _ _ _ _ has had lots of experience. That's the comb God gives you after you've lost your hair.

" _ _ _ _ _ likes company when he parties — how else can he get home drunk?

" _ _ _ _ _ told me: "Experience teaches us you learn nothing from experience."

" _ _ _ _ _ has always been generous. He believes in sharing the credit with the man who did the work.

" _ _ _ _ _ is very fit — he spends his time jumping to conclusions.

" _ _ _ _ _ has suffered all his life from zeal. That's a nervous disorder cured only by experience.

" _ _ _ _ _ has a very traditional mind — he believes nothing should be done for the first time.

" _ _ _ _ _ has children who will be a great comfort in his old age. They should, they helped him get there quickly.

" _ _ _ _ _ has always been a optimist — he can see the benefit of every situation. The rest of us just don't have time to look that hard.

" _ _ _ _ _ believes there are two sides to every question — and he disagrees with both.

" _ _ _ _ _ may not believe he's God — but he pays close attention when he talks to himself.

" _ _ _ _ _ once told me any fool can criticize him, and many do.

" _ _ _ _ _ his wife once told me she caught him drinking before they went out to a party. "Why are you doing that?" He replied, "It's because I don't like to drink on an empty stomach."

" The best advice I can offer tonight is, "Don't ever listen to advice."

Quotes
and proverbs

Ability and achievement

66

Natural abilities are like natural plants that need pruning by study.
FRANCIS BACON

99

Our greatest glory is not in never falling, but in rising every time we fall.
CONFUCIUS

66

Everything comes to him who hustles while he waits.
THOMAS EDISON

99

People are always ready to admit a man's ability after he gets there.
BOB EDWARDS

66

There is something that is much more scarce, something rarer than ability. It is the ability to recognize ability.
ROBERT HALF

99

The only thing some people do is grow older.
ED HOWE

66

God will not look you over for medals, degrees or diplomas, but for scars!
ELBERT HUBBARD

99

The world is divided into people who do things — and people who get the credit.
DWIGHT W. MORROW

66

Ability is the art of getting credit for all the home runs somebody else hits.
CASEY STENGEL

99

You aim for the palace and get drowned in the sewer.
MARK TWAIN

66

To achieve great things we must live as though we were never going to die.
MARQUIS DE VAUVENARGUES

Acting and actors

"

Theater director: a person engaged by the management to conceal the fact that the players cannot act.
JAMES AGATE

"

An actor's success has the life expectancy of a small boy about to look into a gas tank with a lighted match.
FRED ALLEN

"

It's one of the tragic ironies of the theater that only one man in it can count on steady work — the night watchman.
TALLULAH BANKHEAD

"

In the theater the audience want to be surprised — but by things that they expect.
TRISTAN BERNARD

66

I have an agent I trust professionally more than anyone else, but with the best intentions he could put me in the shithouse just as fast as somebody who wanted to ruin me.
JAMES CAAN

99

I'm a skilled, professional actor. Whether I have any talent or not is beside the point.
MICHAEL CAINE

66

My mother was against me being an actress — until I introduced her to Frank Sinatra.
ANGIE DICKINSON

99

Acting is like prizefighting. The downtown gyms are smelly, but that's where the champions are.
KIRK DOUGLAS

66

Being a star is an agent's dream, not an actor's.
ROBERT DUVALL

99

Actors are often thought of as talking props.
EMILIO ESTEVEZ

66

My agent said: "You aren't good enough for movies." I said: "You're fired."
SALLY FIELD

99

Acting is hell: you spend all your time trying to do what they put people in asylums for.
JANE FONDA

66

Actors who are in it for any length of time either evolve into directors or drunks.
GENE HACKMAN

99

Acting is a nice childish profession — pretending you're someone else and, at the same time, selling yourself.
KATHARINE HEPBURN

66

Actresses will happen in the best regulated families.
OLIVER HERFORD

99

I never said all actors are cattle, what I said was all actors should be treated like cattle.
ALFRED HITCHCOCK

❝

Acting is a way of living out one's insanity.
ISABELLE HUPPERT

❞

I'm a charactor actor in a leading man's body.
WILLIAM HURT

❝

*Acting is like making love. It's better if
your partner is good, but it's probably possible
if your partner isn't.*
JEREMY IRONS

❞

*When I have to cry, I think about my love life.
When I have to laugh, I think about my love life.*
GLENDA JACKSON

❝

*You'd think it something one would grow out of.
But you grow into it. The more you do, the more
you realize how painfully easy it is to be lousy and
how very difficult to be good.*
GLENDA JACKSON

❞

*Only difference between me and other actors is
I've spent more time in jail.*
ROBERT MITCHUM

66

I enjoy being a highly overpaid actor.
ROGER MOORE

99

Acting is like letting your pants down:
you're exposed.
PAUL NEWMAN

66

Acting has been described as farting
about in disguise.
PETER O'TOOLE

99

They criticize me: "Why's he doing such muck?"
To pay for three children in school, for
my family, and their future.
LAURENCE OLIVIER

66

What is acting but lying, and what is good
acting but convincing lying?
LAURENCE OLIVIER

99

There are two types: toupee actors
and non-toupee actors.
DONALD PLEASANCE

66

*Someone called actors "sculptors in snow."
Very apt. In the end, it's all nothing.*
VINCENT PRICE

99

*I want to direct two times a year. You can only hold
your stomach in for so many years.*
BURT REYNOLDS

66

*The art of acting consists in keeping
people from coughing.*
RALPH RICHARDSON

99

*I do not want actors and actresses to understand
my plays. If they will only pronounce the correct
sounds I can guarantee the results.*
GEORGE BERNARD SHAW

66

*The play was a great success, but the
audience was a disaster.*
OSCAR WILDE

99

*Acting is like sex. You should do it,
not talk about it.*
JOANNE WOODWARD

Adultery and divorce

"

For a while we pondered whether to take a vacation or get a divorce. We decided that a trip to Bermuda is over in two weeks but a divorce is something you always have.
WOODY ALLEN

"

Acrimony: what a divorced man gives his wife.
ANONYMOUS

"

Alimony: bounty after the mutiny.
ANONYMOUS

"

Divorce is the sacrament of adultery.
ANONYMOUS

"

Do not lengthen the quarrel while there is an opportunity of escaping.
ANONYMOUS

99

Marriage is grounds for divorce.
ANONYMOUS

66

Alimony is like buying oats for a dead horse.
ARTHUR "BUGS" BAER

99

If you were married to Marilyn Monroe —
you'd cheat with some ugly girl.
GEORGE BURNS

66

What men call gallantry, and gods adultery,
Is much more common where the climate's sultry.
LORD BYRON

99

It wasn't exactly a divorce — I was traded.
TIM CONWAY

66

People who commit adultery must die. Everyone
knows that. Any movie tells you that!
RICHARD DREYFUSS

99

He taught me housekeeping; when I divorce
I keep the house.
ZSA ZSA GABOR

66

Divorce is a game played by lawyers.
CARY GRANT

99

*Alimony: the fine for speeding in the
joy-ride of matrimony.*
OLIVER HERFORD AND JOHN CLAY

66

*Wedding: a necessary formality before
securing a divorce.*
OLIVER HERFORD AND JOHN CLAY

99

*You don't know anything about a woman
until you meet her in court.*
NORMAN MAILER

66

*She cried, and the judge wiped her tears
away with my checkbook.*
TOMMY MANVILLE

99

*Eighty percent of married men cheat in America.
The rest cheat in Europe.*
JACKIE MASON

❝

You know, of course, that the Tasmanians, who never committed adultery, are now extinct.
W. SOMERSET MAUGHAM

❞

Honesty has ruined more marriages than infidelity.
CHARLES MCCABE

❝

Why fool around with hamburger when you have steak at home?
PAUL NEWMAN

❞

Love the quest; marriage the conquest; divorce the inquest.
HELEN ROWLAND

❝

One man's folly is another man's wife.
HELEN ROWLAND

❞

A wife lasts only for the length of the marriage, but an ex-wife is there for the rest of your life.
JIM SAMUELS

❝

I cannot mate in captivity.
GLORIA STEINEM (on why she never married)

Advertising

*Advertising works —
last week I advertised for
a security guard and last
night we were burgled.*
ANONYMOUS

*There is no such thing as
bad publicity except your
own obituary.*
BRENDAN BEHAN

*First Law of Wing Walking:
never leave go of what you've got hold of
until you've got hold of something else.*
BERRY AND HOMER, INC.

*Doing business without advertising
is like winking at a girl in the dark:
you know what you are doing,
but no one else does.*
STEWART H. BRITT

66

The philosophy behind much advertising is based on the old observation that every man is really two men — the man he is and the man he wants to be.
WILLIAM FEATHER

99

Advertising — a judicious mixture of flattery and threats.
NORTHROP FRYE

66

A promise, such a promise — that is the soul of any advertisement.
SAMUEL JOHNSON

99

Advertising may be described as the science of arresting human intelligence long enough to get money from it.
STEPHEN LEACOCK

66

You can fool all of the people all of the time if the advertising is right and the budget is big enough.
JOSEPH E. LEVINE

99

Kodak sells film, but they do not advertise film. They advertise memories.
THEODORE LEVITT

66

What kills a skunk is the publicity it gives itself.
ABRAHAM LINCOLN

99

*Ninety-Mile Beach was obviously named by
one of New Zealand's first advertising copywriters
— it's fifty-six miles long.*
JOHN W. MCDERMOTT

66

*Advertising is the greatest art form of
the twentieth century.*
MARSHALL MCLUHAN

99

*Beneath this slab
John Brown is stowed.
He watched the ads,
And not the road.*
OGDEN NASH

66

*The number of agency people
required to shoot a commercial on location
is in direct proportion to the mean temperature
of the location.*
SHELBY PAGE

99

*Buy me and you will overcome the anxieties
I have just reminded you of.*
MICHAEL SCHUDSON

66

*Advertising should enhance the scenery. It has to
be popular and beautiful at the same time.*
JACKY SETTON

99

*Freedom of the press in Britain is freedom to
print such of the proprietor's prejudices as
the advertisers don't object to.*
HANNEN SWAFFER

66

*Many a small thing has been made large
by the right kind of advertising.*
MARK TWAIN

99

Advertising is legalized lying.
H.G. WELLS

66

*In advertising terms, an intellectual is anybody
who reads a morning newspaper.*
ANNA-MARIA WINCHESTER

Aging

66

Life is a hereditary disease.
ANONYMOUS

99

Middle age is when you have the choice of two temptations and choose the one that will get you home earlier.
ANONYMOUS

66

Nostalgia isn't what it used to be.
ANONYMOUS

99

Reality is sometimes good for kicks, but don't let it get you down.
ANONYMOUS

66

The prospect of tomorrow's joy will never console me for today's boredom.
ANONYMOUS

99

There's many a good tune played on an old fiddle.
ANONYMOUS

66

Wrinkles — the service stripes of life.
ANONYMOUS

99

It's sad to grow old, but nice to ripen.
BRIGITTE BARDOT

66

*If I'd known I was gonna live this long (100 years),
I'd have taken better care of myself.*
JAMES HUBERT BLAKE

99

*Old age takes away from us what we have
inherited and gives us what we have earned.*
GERALD BRENAN

66

*When a man is warned to slow down by a
doctor instead of a policeman.*
SIDNEY BRODY (on middle age)

99

*I was brought up to respect my elders and now
I don't have to respect anybody.*
GEORGE BURNS

66

*I'd go out with women my age. But there
are no women my age.*
GEORGE BURNS

99

*A lady of "certain age," which
means "certainly aged."*
LORD BYRON

66

*I've honestly not been too aware of my age
until I went to the doctor for a full check-up.
He said I had the heart of a young man —
"but you're not young, you're forty."*
SEAN CONNERY

99

Gray hair is God's graffiti.
BILL COSBY

66

*They tell you that you'll lose your mind when you
grow older. What they don't tell you is that you
won't miss it very much.*
MALCOLM COWLEY

99

*An actress I knew — when I filmed with her, I
was thirty-one and she was thirty-six. Today, I'm
forty and she's still only thirty-seven.*
TONY CURTIS

66

*The years between fifty and seventy are the hardest.
You are always being asked to do things, and you
are not yet decrepit enough to turn them down.*
T.S. ELIOT

99

*I'm perfect. The areas that I need help on are not
negotiable. They have to do with gravity.*
JANE FONDA

66

*A diplomat is a man who always remembers a
woman's birthday but never remembers her age.*
ROBERT FROST

99

Youth is a disease from which we all recover.
DOROTHY FULDHEIM

66

*When you're my age, you just never risk
being ill — because then everyone says:
"Oh, he's done for."*
SIR JOHN GIELGUD

99

*Middle age is when your age starts to
show around your middle.*
BOB HOPE

66

*You know you're getting old when the
candles cost more than the cake.*
BOB HOPE

99

*Whenever a man's friends begin to compliment
him about looking young, he may be sure that
they think he is growing old.*
WASHINGTON IRVING

66

Few people know how to be old.
LA ROCHEFOUCAULD

99

*I absolutely refuse to reveal my age.
What am I — a car?*
CYNDIE LAUPER

66

*Remember that as a teenager you are in the last
stage of your life when you will be happy to hear
that the phone is for you.*
FRAN LEBOWITZ

99

If God had to give women wrinkles, He might at least have put them on the soles of her feet.
NINON DE LENCLOS

66

I am just turning forty and taking my time about it.
HAROLD LLOYD

99

Age is not all decay; it is the ripening, the swelling, of the fresh life within, that withers and bursts the husk.
GEORGE MACDONALD

66

Youth is a religion from which one always ends up being converted.
ANDRE MALRAUX

99

A man is only as old as the woman he feels.
GROUCHO MARX

66

The best thing about getting old is that all those things you couldn't have when you were young you no longer want.
L.S. McCANDLESS

99

Old age is like a plane flying through a storm.
Once you're aboard there's nothing you can do.
GOLDA MEIR

66

The older I grow the more I distrust the familiar
doctrine that age brings wisdom.
H.L. MENCKEN

99

Maturity is behavior determined by the
plans other people have in mind.
DAVID MERCER

66

Middle age is when you're sitting at home on
Saturday night and the telephone rings and you
hope it isn't for you.
OGDEN NASH

99

The older you get, the faster you ran as a kid.
STEVE OWEN

66

How old would you be if you didn't
know how old you are?
SATCHELL PAIGE

99

Don't worry about middle age: you'll outgrow it.
LAURENCE J. PETER

66

*Middle age is when anything new in the way
you feel is most likely a symptom.*
LAURENCE J. PETER

99

*Middle age is when the best
exercise is one of discretion.*
LAURENCE J. PETER

66

*Men are like wine — some turn to
vinegar, but the best improve with age.*
POPE JOHN XXIII

99

*Growing old is like being increasingly penalized
for a crime you haven't committed.*
ANTHONY POWELL

66

*I am delighted to be with you. In fact, at my age,
I am delighted to be anywhere.*
RONALD REAGAN

99

*Oh, to be only half as wonderful as my child
thought I was when he was small, and only half as
stupid as my teenager now thinks I am.*
REBECCA RICHARDS

66

I'm in pretty good shape for the shape I'm in.
MICKEY ROONEY

99

*First you forget names, then you forget faces,
then you forget to pull your zipper up, then
you forget to pull your zipper down.*
LEO ROSENBURG

66

*As I grow older and older
And totter towards the tomb
I find I care less and less
Who goes to bed with whom.*
DOROTHY L. SAYERS

99

*The first forty years of life give us the text; the
next thirty supply the commentary on it.*
ARTHUR SCHOPENHAUER

❝

When a man retires and time is no longer a matter of urgent importance, his colleagues generally present him with a watch.
R.C. SHERRIFF

❞

I see a body as a classy chassis to carry your mind around in.
SYLVESTER STALLONE

❝

No one is twenty-two. I've got shoes older than that.
SYLVESTER STALLONE

❞

Old men and comets have been reverenced for the same reason: their long beards and pretences to foretell events.
JONATHAN SWIFT

❝

I'm sixty-five and I guess that puts me in with the geriatrics, but if there were fifteen months in every year, I'd only be forty-eight.
JAMES THURBER

❞

Life begins at forty.
SOPHIE TUCKER

Alcohol

66

I'm so holy that when I touch wine it turns to water.
AGA KHAN III

Everybody should believe in something. I believe I'll have another drink.
ANONYMOUS

66

I love my wife. She drives me to drink — and back afterward.
ANONYMOUS

99

Somewhere in the limbo which divides perfect sobriety from mild intoxication.
CYRIL ASQUITH

66

One reason I don't drink is that I want to know when I'm having a good time.
NANCY ASTOR

99

*The trouble with the world is that it's
always one drink behind.*
HUMPHREY BOGART

66

*I have taken more out of alcohol than
alcohol has taken out of me.*
WINSTON CHURCHILL

99

*Some men are like musical glasses; to produce
their finest tones you must keep them wet.*
SAMUEL TAYLOR COLERIDGE

66

*A man shouldn't fool with booze until he's fifty;
then he's a damn fool if he doesn't.*
WILLIAM FAULKNER

99

*A woman drove me to drink, and I never even
had the courtesy to thank her.*
W.C. FIELDS

66

*I always keep a supply of stimulant handy in case
I see a snake — which I also keep handy.*
W.C. FIELDS

99

Once, during Prohibition, I was forced to live for days on nothing but food and water.
W.C. FIELDS

66

Wine is constant proof that God loves us and wants us to be happy.
BENJAMIN FRANKLIN

99

If you resolve to give up smoking, drinking, and loving, you don't actually live longer; it just seems longer.
CLEMENT FREUD

66

Drinking removes warts and pimples. Not from me. But from those I look at.
JACKIE GLEASON

99

I have never been drunk, but I have often been overserved.
GEORGE GOBEL

66

Beer makes you feel as you ought to feel without beer.
HENRY LAWSON

99

I don't drink liquor. I don't like it.
It makes me feel good.
OSCAR LEVANT

66

I always wake up at the crack of ice.
JOE E. LEWIS

99

Love makes the world go round? Not at all.
Whiskey makes it go round twice as fast.
COMPTON MACKENZIE

66

Prohibition makes you want to cry into your beer
and denies you the beer to cry into.
DON MARQUIS

99

You're not drunk if you can lie on the
floor without holding on.
DEAN MARTIN

66

I've made it a rule never to drink by daylight
and never to refuse a drink after dark.
H.L. MENCKEN

99

*I try not to drink too much because
when I'm drunk, I bite.*
BETTE MIDLER

66

*Diogenes was asked what wine he liked best;
and he answered as I would have done when
he said: "Somebody else's."*
MICHEL DE MONTAIGNE

99

I drink to make other people more interesting.
GEORGE JEAN NATHAN

66

*An Irish queer: a fellow who
prefers women to drink.*
SEAN O'FAOLAIN

99

One more drink and I'd have been under the host.
DOROTHY PARKER

66

I drink no more than a sponge.
RABELAIS

99

Work is the curse of the drinking classes.
MIKE ROMANOFF

66

*Alcohol is the anesthesia by which we
endure the operation of life.*
GEORGE BERNARD SHAW

99

But I'm not so think as you drunk I am.
J.C. SQUIRE

66

When asked if he had a drinking problem:
"Yes, there's never enough."
DENIS THATCHER

99

*An alcoholic is a man you don't like
who drinks as much as you do.*
DYLAN THOMAS

66

*I don't have a drink problem
except when I can't get one.*
TOM WAITS

99

*I hadn't the heart to touch my breakfast.
I told Jeeves to drink it himself.*
P.G. WODEHOUSE

Alcohol: proverbs

A good drink makes the old young.

A rash man, a skin of good wine, and a glass vessel, do not last long.

Better weak beer than an empty cask.

Drink less and go home by daylight.

Drink nothing without seeing it, sign nothing without reading it.

Drinking water neither makes a man sick, nor in debt, nor his wife a widow.

Drunkards and fools cannot lie.

Drunkenness does not produce faults, it discovers them.

He that buys land buys many stones; he that buys flesh buys many bones; he that buys eggs buys many shells; but he that buys good ale buys nothing else.

He that goes to bed thirsty, rises healthy.

He who drinks a little too much drinks much too much.

The first glass for thirst, the second for nourishment, the third for pleasure, and the fourth for madness.

There are more old drunkards than old doctors.

Thousands drink themselves to death before one dies of thirst.

Under a shabby coat may be a smart drinker.

What is sweet in the mouth is not always good for the stomach.

What the sober man thinks, the drunkard tells.

When everybody says you are drunk, go to sleep.

Wine upon beer is very good cheer, beer upon wine consider with fear.

Ambition

66

The nail that sticks up gets hammered down.
ANONYMOUS

99

Ah, but a man's reach should exceed his grasp, Or what's a heaven for?
ROBERT BROWNING

66

I have found some of the best reasons I ever had for remaining at the bottom by looking at the men at the top.
FRANK MORE COLBY

66

Men who never get carried away should be.
MALCOLM FORBES

99

One can never consent to creep when one feels an impulse to soar.
HELEN KELLER

66

*When people inquire I always just state,
"I have four nice children, and hope to have
eight."*
ALINE MURRAY KILMER

99

*If you aren't fired with enthusiasm, you will be fired
with enthusiasm.*
VINCE LOMBARDI

66

*Most people would succeed in small things if they
were not troubled with great ambitions.*
HENRY WADSWORTH LONGFELLOW

99

*Ours is a world where people don't know what they
want and are willing to go through hell to get it.*
DON MARQUIS

66

I was going to buy a copy of The Power of Positive
Thinking, *and then I thought: what the hell good
would that do?*
RONNIE SHAKES

99

*The biggest things are always the easiest to do
because there is no competition.*
WILLIAM VAN HORNE

America and Americans

"
*California is a great
place — if you happen
to be an orange.*
FRED ALLEN

"
*Hollywood: the place
where girls go to look for
husbands and husbands
go to look for girls.*
ANONYMOUS

"
*In America, you watch TV and think that's totally
unreal, then you step outside and it's just the same.*
JOAN ARMATRADING

"
I love New York City. I've got a gun.
CHARLES BARKLEY

"
*Whoever wants to know the hearts and minds of
America had better learn baseball.*
JACQUES BARZUN

❝

Americans are broad-minded people. They'll accept the fact that a person can be an alcoholic, a dope fiend, and a wife beater, and even a newspaperman, but if a man doesn't drive there's something wrong with him.
ART BUCHWALD

❞

People who break their word in Japan kill themselves. People who break their word here kill you.
MICHAEL CAINE (on Hollywood)

❝

In California everyone goes to a therapist, is a therapist, or is a therapist going to a therapist.
TRUMAN CAPOTE

❞

It is a scientific fact that if you stay in California you lose one point off your IQ every year.
TRUMAN CAPOTE

❝

America is the only nation in history that miraculously has gone from barbarism to degeneration without the usual interval of civilization.
GEORGES CLEMENCEAU

99

*When asked by an anthropologist what the
Indians called America before the white man
came, an Indian said simply, "Ours."*
VINE DELORIA, JR.

66

Living in Hollywood is like living in a lit cigar butt.
PHYLLIS DILLER

99

*The thing that impresses me the most about
Americans is the way parents obey their children.*
DUKE OF WINDSOR (EDWARD VIII)

66

*Hollywood: the only place in the world
where a man gets stabbed in the back
while climbing a ladder.*
WILLIAM FAULKNER

99

America is a mistake, a giant mistake!
SIGMUND FREUD

66

*Americans are like a rich father who wishes
he knew how to give his son the hardships
that made him rich.*
ROBERT FROST

99

The United States is like a gigantic boiler. Once the fire is lighted under it there's no limit to the power it can generate.
LORD GREY

66

The city of Brotherly Shove.
O. HENRY (on New York City)

99

It's an American characteristic not to stop running even after you have arrived.
CLIVE JAMES

66

America never stands taller than when her people go down on their knees.
LYNDON B. JOHNSON

99

The United States has to move very fast to even stand still.
JOHN F. KENNEDY

66

I spent two miserable years in California. But it was Barbara Stanwyck who said: "The best place to be miserable is California."
ANDREI KONCHALOVSKY

99

This is the most exciting place in the world to live.
There are so many ways to die here.
DENIS LEARY (on New York City)

66

Florida: God's waiting room.
GLENN LE GRICE

99

Strip away the phony tinsel of Hollywood and you
will find the real tinsel underneath.
OSCAR LEVANT

66

There's nothing wrong with Southern California
that a rise in the ocean level wouldn't cure.
ROSS MACDONALD

99

There's no underestimating the intelligence
of the American public.
H.L. MENCKEN

66

America may be violent, greedy, and colonialist
but my God, it's interesting.
PAUL NEWMAN

99

The Americans don't really understand what's going on in Bosnia. To them it's the unspellables killing the unpronounceables.
P.J. O'ROURKE

66

The American political system is like fast food — mushy, insipid, made out of disgusting parts of things, and everybody wants some.
P.J. O'ROURKE

99

America is a country that doesn't know where it is going but is determined to set a speed record getting there.
LAURENCE J. PETER

66

If you stay in Beverly Hills too long you become a Mercedes.
ROBERT REDFORD

99

In Hollywood, if you don't have happiness you send out for it.
REX REED

66

*The difference between Los Angeles and yogurt
is that yogurt has real culture.*
TOM TAUSSIK

99

*America is a large, friendly dog in a very
small room. Every time it wags its tail it
knocks over a chair.*
ARNOLD TOYNBEE

66

*America: the only country in the world
where failing to promote yourself is
regarded as being arrogant.*
GARRY TRUDEAU

99

The White House is the finest jail in the world.
HARRY S. TRUMAN

66

*It was wonderful to find America, but it
would have been more wonderful to miss it.*
MARK TWAIN

99

*America is somewhat like Palestine before Christ
appeared — a country full of minor prophets.*
PETER USTINOV

66

In America, through pressure of conformity, there is freedom of choice, but nothing to choose from.
PETER USTINOV

99

Suburbia is where the developer bulldozes out the trees, then names the streets after them.
BILL VAUGHAN

66

That's the old American way — if you've got a good thing, then overdo it.
PHIL WALDEN

99

California is a mess. Closet neuroticism is all very well; elevated to an art form it's rather tiresome.
MICHAEL WATKINS

66

It is absurd to say that there are neither ruins nor curiosities in America when they have their mothers and their manners.
OSCAR WILDE

99

Of course, America had often been discovered before Columbus, but it had always been hushed up.
OSCAR WILDE

Ancestry

❝

I don't have to look up my family tree, because I know that I'm the sap.
FRED ALLEN

❞

A genealogist is one who traces your family back as far as your money will go.
ANONYMOUS

❝

Good wine needs no vine.
ANONYMOUS

❞

A degenerate nobleman, or one that is proud of his birth, is like a turnip. There is nothing good of him but that which is underground.
SAMUEL BUTLER

❝

Gentility is what is left over from rich ancestors after the money is gone.
JOHN CIARDI

99

I can trace my ancestry back to a protoplasmal primordial atomic globule. Consequently, my family pride is something inconceivable.
W.S. GILBERT

66

None of us can boast about the morality of our ancestors. The records do not show that Adam and Eve were married.
ED HOWE

99

The difference between us is that my family begins with me, whereas yours ends with you.
IPHICRATES

66

I don't know who my grandfather was; I am much more concerned to know what his grandson will be.
ABRAHAM LINCOLN

99

We pay for the mistakes of our ancestors and it seems only fair that they should leave us the money to pay with.
DON MARQUIS

Animals

66

*The lion and the calf shall
lie down together but the
calf won't get much sleep.*
WOODY ALLEN

99

*I've been teaching my dog
to beg. Last night he came
home with 20 dollars.*
ANONYMOUS

66

*Every day my dog and I go for a tramp in the
woods. The dog loves it, but the tramp is getting
a bit fed up.*
ANONYMOUS

99

*Mouse: an animal which strews its path with
fainting women.*
AMBROSE BIERCE

66

*Money will buy a pretty good dog but it won't buy
the wag in his tail.*
JOSH BILLINGS

99

*Dogs come when they are called; cats take a
message and get back to you.*
MARY BLY

66

*The great pleasure of a dog is that you may make a
fool of yourself with him and not only will he not
scold you, he will make a fool of himself too.*
SAMUEL BUTLER

99

*To err is human
To purr feline.*
ROBERT BYRNE

66

*Whenever you observe an animal closely,
you feel as if a human being sitting inside
were making fun of you.*
ELIAS CANETTI

99

When turkeys mate they think of swans.
JOHNNY CARSON

66

*I like pigs. Dogs look up to us. Cats look down
on us. Pigs treat us as equals.*
WINSTON CHURCHILL

99

*Mankind differs from the animals only by a little —
and most people throw that away.*
CONFUCIUS

66

*Great fleas have little fleas upon
their backs to bite em,
And little fleas have lesser fleas,
and so ad infinitum.*
AUGUSTUS DE MORGAN

99

*The clever cat eats cheese,
then breathes down rat holes
with baited breath.*
W.C. FIELDS

66

*An elephant — a mouse built to government
specifications.*
ROBERT HEINLEIN

99

*The dog, to gain some private ends,
went mad and bit the man.
The man recovered from the bite.
The dog it was that died.*
GARRISON KEILLOR

66

Cats are intended to teach us that not everything in nature has a function.
GARRISON KEILLOR

99

Spiders are the SAS of nature, and will spend hours flying through the air on their ropes, prior to landing and subjecting some hapless insect to savage interrogation. The question they usually ask is: "Have you any last requests?"
MILES KINGTON

66

Cats seem to go on the principle that it never does any harm to ask for what you want.
JOSEPH WOOD KRUTCH

99

A dog is like a liberal. He wants to please everybody. A cat really doesn't need to know that everybody loves him.
WILLIAM KUNSTLER

66

I distrust camels, and anyone else who can go a week without a drink.
JOE E. LEWIS

99

A zoo is a place of refuge where savage beasts are protected from people.
GERALD F. LIEBERMAN

66

Oh, a wondrous bird is the pelican!
His beak holds more than his belican.
He takes in his beak
Food enough for a week.
But I'll be darned if I know how the helican.
DIXON LANIER MERRITT

99

One disadvantage of being a hog is that at any moment some blundering fool may try to make a silk purse out of your wife's ear.
J.B. MORTON

66

The camel has a single hump;
The dromedary, two;
Or else the other way around,
I'm never sure. Are you?
OGDEN NASH

99

I loathe people who keep dogs. They are cowards who haven't got the guts to bite people themselves.
AUGUST STRINDBERG

"

*Often it does seem a pity that Noah and his party
did not miss the boat.*
MARK TWAIN

"

*Cats are smarter than dogs. You can't get eight cats
to pull a sled through snow.*
JEFF VALDEZ

"

*We hope that, when the insects take over the world,
they will remember with gratitude how we took
them along on all our picnics.*
BILL VAUGHAN

"

*Animals have these advantages over man
. . . they have no theologians to instruct them, . . .
their funerals cost them nothing, and no one starts
lawsuits over their wills.*
VOLTAIRE

"

Cocker Spaniel Annual Manual
LUTHER VRETTOS (on a suggested magazine title)

"

*If a dog jumps onto your lap it is because he is
fond of you; but if a cat does the same thing it is
because your lap is warmer.*
ALFRED NORTH WHITEHEAD

Appearance

"

All that glitters is not gold.
ANONYMOUS

"

Among the blind the one-eyed man is king.
ANONYMOUS

"

Her face looks as if it had worn out two bodies.
ANONYMOUS

"

In Italy a woman can have a face like a train wreck if she's blonde.
ANONYMOUS

"

You can't tell a book by its cover.
ANONYMOUS

"

My face looks like a wedding cake left out in the rain.
W.H. AUDEN

"

The only hope for someone like me with pigeon toes is that one day, I'll be carried off feet first in a flight of my own fancy.
ALAN AYCKBOURN

"

She was what we used to call a suicide blond — dyed by her own hand.
SAUL BELLOW

"

He had the sort of face that makes you realize God does have a sense of humor.
BILL BRYSON

"

The expression a woman wears on her face is more important than the clothes she wears on her back.
DALE CARNEGIE

"

Sunburn is very becoming — but only when it is even — one must be careful not to look like a mixed grill.
NOEL COWARD

"

The most delightful advantage of being bald — one can hear snowflakes.
R.G. DANIELS

66

*It's a good thing that beauty is only skin deep, or
I'd be rotten to the core.*
PHYLLIS DILLER

99

*When I go to the beauty parlor, I always use the
emergency entrance. Sometimes I just go for an
estimate.*
PHYLLIS DILLER

66

*We have two ears and one tongue in order that we
may hear more and speak less.*
DIOGENES

99

*Things are seldom what they seem,
Skim milk masquerades as cream.*
W.S. GILBERT

66

There's one thing about baldness — it's neat.
DON HEROLD

99

*His ears make him look like a taxi cab with both
doors open.*
HOWARD HUGHES (of Clark Gable)

❝

*A man who so much resembled a Baked Alaska —
sweet, warm and sticky on the outside, hard and
cold within.*
FRANCIS KING (of C.P. Snow)

❞

*Sometimes when you look in his eyes you get the
feeling that someone else is driving.*
DAVID LETTERMAN

❝

*A smile that snapped back after using. like a
stretched rubber band.*
SINCLAIR LEWIS

❞

*The Lord prefers common-looking people. That's
why he makes so many of them.*
ABRAHAM LINCOLN

❝

He looks as if he had been weaned on a pickle.
ALICE ROOSEVELT LONGWORTH

❞

*I never forget a face, but I'll make an exception in
your case.*
GROUCHO MARX

66

She got her good looks from her father. He's a plastic surgeon.
GROUCHO MARX

99

Beauty is only skin deep, but ugly goes clear to the bone.
MURPHY'S LAW

66

I'd like to borrow his body for just 48 hours. There are three guys I'd like to beat up and four women I'd like to make love to.
JIM MURRAY

99

*Men seldom make passes
At girls who wear glasses.*
DOROTHY PARKER

66

I never expected to see the day when girls would get sunburned in the places they do today.
WILL ROGERS

99

I always say beauty is only sin deep.
SAKI

66

He had a winning smile, but everything else was a loser.
GEORGE C. SCOTT

99

The body of a young woman is God's greatest achievement . . . Of course, He could have made it to last longer but you can't have everything.
NEIL SIMON

66

A short neck denotes a good mind . . . You see, the messages go quicker to the brain because they've shorter to go.
MURIEL SPARK

99

. . . the sort of eye that can open an oyster at sixty paces.
P.G. WODEHOUSE

66

There is only one cure for grey hair. It was invented by a Frenchman. It is called the guillotine.
P.G. WODEHOUSE

99

Why don't you get a haircut; you look like a chrysanthemum.
P.G. WODEHOUSE

Appearance: proverbs

A good face is a letter of recommendation.

An envious man's face grows sharp; his eyes big.

Appearances are deceptive.

A whore in a fine dress is like a clean entrance to a dirty house.

Bees that have honey in their mouths have stings in their tails.

Better a slip of the foot than the tongue.

Beware of one who flatters unduly; he will also criticize unjustly.

Confidence generates confidence.

Fools invent fashions that wise men will wear.

Good clothes open all doors.

If not for the belly, the back might wear gold.

People often change, and seldom for the better.

Power often goes before talent.

Rich garments weep on unworthy shoulders.

Straight trees have crooked roots.

The Italians are wise before the act, the Germans in the act, the French after the act.

Things are not always what they seem.

Truth has a good face, but bad clothes.

Ugly women, finely dressed, are the uglier for it.

Under a ragged coat lies wisdom.

Vanity has no greater foe than vanity.

Vice is often clothed in virtue's habit.

When the host smiles most blandly he has an eye to the guest's purse.

Architecture

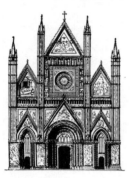

66

In my experience, if you have to keep the lavatory door shut by extending your left leg, it's modern architecture.
NANCY BANKS-SMITH

99

Architect. One who drafts a plan of your house, and plans a draft of your money.
AMBROSE BIERCE

66

The relationship between architects and the media is based on trust and understanding. The architects don't trust the media and the media don't understand the architects.
BUILDING DESIGN MAGAZINE

99

You have to give this much to the Luftwaffe: when it knocked down our buildings it did not replace them with anything more offensive than rubble. We did that.
CHARLES, PRINCE OF WALES

"

The Stately Homes of England,
How beautiful they stand,
To prove the upper classes,
Have still the upper hand.
NOEL COWARD

"

Architecture is the art of how to waste space.
PHILIP JOHNSON

"

Post-war architecture is the accountant's revenge
on the pre-war businessman's dreams.
REM KOOLHAAS

"

Architecture begins when you place two bricks
carefully *together.*
MIES VAN DER ROHE

"

Suburbia is where the developer bulldozes out the
trees, then names the streets after them.
BILL VAUGHAN

"

The doctor can bury his mistakes but an architect
can only advise his client to plant vines.
FRANK LLOYD WRIGHT

Argument

❝

Our disputants put me in mind of the skuttle fish, that when he is unable to extricate himself, blackens all the water about him, till he becomes invisible.
JOSEPH ADDISON

❞

He always had a chip on his shoulder that he was ready to use to kindle an argument.
FRED ALLEN

❝

Silence is one of the hardest things to refute.
JOSH BILLINGS

❞

Thrice is he armed that hath his quarrel just, but four times he who gets his blows in fust.
JOSH BILLINGS

❝

When your argument has little or no substance, abuse your oponent.
CICERO

99

Those who in quarrels interpose,
Must often wipe a bloody nose.
JOHN GAY

66

I always get the better when I argue alone.
OLIVER GOLDSMITH

99

No matter what side of an argument you're on, you
always find some people on your side that you wish
were on the other side.
JASCHA HEIFETZ

66

An argument always leaves each party convinced
that the other has a closed mind.
LAURENCE J. PETER

99

There are two sides to every argument, until you
take one.
LAURENCE J. PETER

66

I am not arguing with you — I am telling you.
JAMES WHISTLER

Art

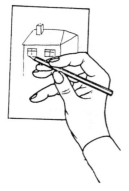

99

He was the world's only armless sculptor. He put the chisel in his mouth and his wife hit him on the back of the head with a mallet.
FRED ALLEN

66

It's easy to understand modern art: if it hangs on the wall it's a painting, if you can walk around it it's a sculpture.
ANONYMOUS

99

Modern art is when you buy a picture to cover a hole in the wall and then decide that the hole looks much better.
ANONYMOUS

66

Buy old masters. They fetch a much better price than old mistresses.
LORD BEAVERBROOK

99

Painting: the art of protecting flat surfaces from the weather and exposing them to the critic.
AMBROSE BIERCE

66

Rembrandt painted about 700 pictures — of these, 3,000 are in existence.
WILHELM BODE

99

Abstract art: a product of the untalented sold by the unprincipled to the utterly bewildered.
AL CAPP

66

Artistic temperament is a disease that afflicts amateurs.
G.K. CHESTERTON

99

Modern art is what happens when painters stop looking at girls and persuade themselves that they have a better idea.
JOHN CIARDI

66

There are only two styles of portrait painting: the serious and the smirk.
CHARLES DICKENS

99

Artists can color the sky red because they know it's blue. The rest of us, who aren't artists, must color things the way they really are, or people might think we're stupid.
JULES FEIFFER

66

I always suspect an artist who is successful before he is dead.
JOHN MURRAY GIBBON

99

*As my poor father used to say
In 1863, Once people start on all this Art
Goodbye moralitee!*
A.P. HERBERT

66

It does not matter how badly you paint so long as you don't paint badly like other people.
GEORGE MOORE

99

A primitive artist is an amateur whose work sells.
GRANDMA MOSES

66

My tutor does watercolors; they are like the work of a girl of fourteen — when she was twelve.
BEN NICHOLSON

99

Two boys arrived yesterday with a pebble they said was the head of a dog until I pointed out that it was really a typewriter.
PABLO PICASSO

66

Artists, by definition innocent, don't steal. But they do borrow without giving back.
NED ROREM

99

An amateur is an artist who supports himself with outside jobs which enable him to paint. A professional is someone whose wife works to enable him to paint.
BEN SHAHN

66

This is either a forgery or a damn clever original!
FRANK SULLIVAN

99

The poetic school of artists who imagine that the true way of idealising a sitter is to paint someone else.
OSCAR WILDE

66

Public art is art that the public can't avoid.
GEORGE WYLLIE

Books and reading

❝

*The best part of the fiction
in many novels is the
notice that the characters
are purely imaginary.*
FRANKLIN P. ADAMS

❞

*Science fiction is no more
written for scientists
than ghost stories are
written for ghosts.*
BRIAN ALDISS

❝

I took a speed reading course and read War and
Peace *in twenty minutes. It involves Russia.*
WOODY ALLEN

❞

*Some books are to be tasted, others to be
swallowed, and some few to
be chewed and digested.*
FRANCIS BACON

❝

*When I am dead, I hope it may be said:
"His sins were scarlet, but his books were read."*
HILAIRE BELLOC

99

*A bestseller was a book which somehow sold well
simply because it was selling well.*
DANIEL J. BOORSTIN

66

Book lovers never go to bed alone.
DANIEL J. BOORSTIN

99

*Never lend books — nobody ever returns them;
the only books I have in my library are those
which people have lent me.*
DANIEL J. BOORSTIN

66

*Reading someone else's newspaper is like
sleeping with someone else's wife. Nothing seems to
be precisely in the right place, and when you
find what you're looking for, it is not clear
then how to respond to it.*
MALCOLM BRADBURY

99

*To read without reflecting is like
eating without digesting.*
EDMUND BURKE

66

A good novel tells us the truth about its hero; but a bad novel tells us the truth about its author.
G.K. CHESTERTON

99

The paperback is very interesting, but I find it will never replace a hardcover book — it makes a very poor doorstop.
ALFRED HITCHCOCK

66

I love to lose myself in other men's minds. When I am not walking, I am reading.
CHARLES LAMB

99

Far too many relied on the classic formula of a beginning, a muddle, and an end.
PHILIP LARKIN (on modern novels)

66

I'm re-reading it with a slow deliberate carelessness.
T.E. LAWRENCE

99

Having your book turned into a movie is like seeing your oxen turned into bouillon cubes.
JOHN LE CARRÉ

"

*When the late President Kennedy was revealed
as a speed reader, it took me three hours to
read the article about it.*
OSCAR LEVANT

"

Book: what they make a movie out of for television.
LEONARD LOUIS LEVINSON

"

*This is not a novel to be tossed aside lightly.
It should be thrown with great force.*
DOROTHY PARKER

"

A library is thought in cold storage.
LORD SAMUEL

"

Reading is to the mind what exercise is to the body.
RICHARD STEELE

"

A novel is a mirror walking along a main road.
STENDHAL

"

*A classic: something that everybody wants to
have read and nobody wants to read.*
MARK TWAIN

Bores

❝

He's the kind of bore who's here today and here tomorrow.
BINNIE BARNES

❞

A bore is a person who talks when you want him to listen.
AMBROSE BIERCE

❝

Society is now one polished horde,
Formed of two mighty tribes,
The Bores and Bored.
LORD BYRON

❞

A bore is a man who deprives you of solitude without providing you with company.
GIAN VINCENZO CRAVINA

❝

Some people can stay longer in an hour than others can in a week.
W.D. HOWELLS

99

A bore is a fellow talker who can change the subject to his topic of conversation faster than you can change it back to yours.
LAURENCE J. PETER

66

Bore: a person who lights up a room simply by leaving it.
LAURENCE J. PETER

99

The worst thing about a bore is not that he won't stop talking, but that he won't let you stop listening.
LAURENCE J. PETER

66

A bore is a man who, when you ask him how he is, tells you.
BERT LESTON TAYLOR

99

He is an old bore; even the grave yawns for him.
HERBERT BEERBOHM TREE

66

A healthy male adult bore consumes one and a half times his own weight in other people's patience.
JOHN UPDIKE

Britain and the British

66

The English instinctively admire any man who has no talent and is modest about it.
JAMES AGATE

99

In England there are sixty different religions, and only one sauce.
DOMENICO CARACCIOLO

66

The English never draw a line without blurring it.
WINSTON CHURCHILL

99

They are the only people who like to be told how bad things are — who like to be told the worst.
WINSTON CHURCHILL (on the British)

66

Anyone who has been to an English public school and served in the British Army is quite at home in a Third World prison.
ROGER COOPER

99

The English think that incompetence is the same thing as sincerity.
QUENTIN CRISP

66

No one can be as calculatedly rude as the British, which amazes Americans, who do not understand studied insult and can only offer abuse as a substitute.
PAUL GALLICO

99

Britain is the only country in the world where being "too clever by half" is an insult.
A. A. GILL

66

One of the freedoms of the English is freedom from culture.
LORD GOODMAN

99

The English never smash in a face. They merely refrain from asking it to dinner.
MARGARET HALSEY

❝

The British have never been a spiritually minded people, so they invented cricket to give them some notion of eternity.
LORD MANCROFT

❞

Britain is the only country in the world where the food is more dangerous than the sex.
JACKIE MASON

❝

One matter Englishmen don't think in the least funny is their happy consciousness of possessing a deep sense of humor.
MARSHALL MCLUHAN

❞

An Englishman, even if he is alone, forms an orderly queue of one.
GEORGE MIKES

❝

The reason nobody talks in England is because children are taught manners instead of conversation.
ROBERT MORLEY

99

England is a nation of shopkeepers.
NAPOLEON BONAPARTE

66

*The Englishman has all the qualities of a poker
except its occasional warmth.*
DANIEL O'CONNELL

99

*The English woman is so refined
She has no bosom and no behind.*
STEVIE SMITH

66

*I know why the sun never sets on the
British Empire — God wouldn't trust an
Englishman in the dark.*
DUNCAN SPAETH

99

The English think soap is civilization.
HEINRICH VON TREITSCHKE

66

*The English have an extraordinary ability for
flying into a great calm.*
ALEXANDER WOOLLCOTT

Business

"

*Business without profit
is not business any more
than a pickle is a candy.*
CHARLES F. ABBOTT

"

*A memorandum is
written not to inform
the reader but to
protect the writer.*
DEAN ACHESON

"

*Supermarkets . . . symbols of man's
inhumanity to women.*
PHILIP ADAMS

"

*Committee — a group of men who individually
can do nothing but as a group decide that
nothing can be done.*
FRED ALLEN

"

*Business is so bad, even the accounts that don't
intend to pay ain't buying.*
ANONYMOUS

99

Let the buyer beware.
ANONYMOUS

66

*To get ten percent out of some businessmen you
have to be a fifty-fifty partner.*
ANONYMOUS

99

*Today's sales should be better than yesterday's —
and worse than tomorrow's.*
ANONYMOUS

66

Where there is a sea there are pirates.
ANONYMOUS

99

*Anyone can cut prices, but it takes brains to
produce a better article.*
P.D. ARMOUR

66

*Bureaucracy is a giant mechanism operated
by pygmies.*
HONORÉ DE BALZAC

99

Generous people make bad shopkeepers.
HONORÉ DE BALZAC

66

*Corporation: an ingenious device
for obtaining individual profit
without individual responsibility.*
AMBROSE BIERCE

99

*Credit . . . is the only enduring testimonial
to man's confidence in man.*
JAMES BLISH

66

*If you hype something and it succeeds,
you're a genius, it wasn't a hype. If you hype
something and it fails, then it's just a hype.*
NEIL BOGART

99

*At some time in the life cycle of virtually
every organization, its ability to succeed in
spite of itself runs out.*
RICHARD H. BRIEN

66

*A business must have a conscience as
well as a counting house.*
MONTAGUE BURTON

99

*Business is a good game — lots of
competition and a minimum of rules.
You keep score with money.*
NOLAN BUSHNELL

66

*Net — the biggest word in the
language of business.*
HERBERT CASSON

99

*The fact that a business is large,
efficient, and profitable does not mean it
takes advantage of the public.*
CHARLES CLORE

66

*A committee is a cul-de-sac down which ideas are
lured and then quietly strangled.*
BARNETT COCKS

99

The business of America is business.
CALVIN COOLIDGE

66

*When business is bad always start weeding
at the top.*
GRAHAM DAY

99

It is well known what a middleman is; he is a man who bamboozles one party and plunders the others.
BENJAMIN DISRAELI

66

Business? it's quite simple: it's other people's money.
ALEXANDER DUMAS (the younger)

99

If you don't drive your business you will be driven out of business.
B.C. FORBES

66

There is more credit and satisfaction in being a first-rate truck driver than a tenth-rate executive.
B.C. FORBES

99

A business that makes nothing but money is a poor kind of business.
HENRY FORD

66

Business will get better, but we won't know it when it does.
HENRY FORD

99

Remember that time is money.
BENJAMIN FRANKLIN

66

*The salary of the chief executive of the large
corporation is not a market award for achievement.
It is frequently in the nature of a warm personal
gesture by the individual to himself.*
J.K. GALBRAITH

99

*A verbal contract isn't worth the paper
it's written on.*
SAM GOLDWYN

66

*Business succeeds rather better than the state in
imposing its restraints upon individuals, because its
imperatives are disguised as choices.*
WALTON HAMILTON

99

*What is a committee? A group of the unwilling,
picked from the unfit, to do the unnecessary.*
RICHARD LONG HARKNESS

66

*The first myth of management is that it exists.
The second myth of management is that
success equals skill.*
ROBERT HELLER

99

*It is just as important that business keep
out of government as that government keep
out of business.*
HERBERT HOOVER

66

A camel is a horse designed by a committee.
ALEC ISSIGONIS

99

*When you are skinning your customers, you
should leave some skin on to grow so that you
can skin them again.*
NIKITA KHRUSHCHEV

66

*The aim of commerce is not to sell what
is best for people, or even what they really
need, but simply to sell; its final standard
is a successful sale.*
RICHARD LIVINGSTONE

99

*Love your neighbor is not merely sound
Christianity; it is good business.*
DAVID LLOYD GEORGE

66

*The oppressed are allowed once every few years to
decide which particular representatives of the
oppressing class are to represent and repress them.*
KARL MARX (on capitalism)

99

*The only thing that saves us from bureaucracy
is its inefficiency.*
EUGENE MCCARTHY

66

*Nobody talks more of free enterprise and
competition and the best man winning than the
man who inherited his father's store or farm.*
C. WRIGHT MILLS

99

*The ideal committee is one with me as chairman,
and two other members in bed with flu.*
LORD MILVERTON

66

*When you've got them by their wallets, their hearts
and minds will follow.*
FERN NAITO

99

*The secret of business is to know something
that nobody else knows.*
ARISTOTLE ONASSIS

66

*Bureaucracy defends the status quo long past the
time when the quo has lost its status.*
LAURENCE J. PETER

99

*We trained hard . . . but every time we were
beginning to form up into teams, we would be
reorganized. I was to learn later in life that we tend
to meet any new situation by reorganizing . . . and
a wonderful method it can be for creating the
illusion of progress while producing inefficiency
and demoralization.*
PETRONIUS

66

*Executive ability is deciding quickly and getting
somebody else to do the work.*
J.C. POLLARD

99

*He's a businessman. I'll make him an offer
he can't refuse.*
MARIO PUZO

66

In the factory we make cosmetics.
In the store we sell hope.
CHARLES REVSON

99

A holding company is the people you give your
money to while you're being searched.
WILL ROGERS

66

There is hardly anything in the world that
some man cannot make a little worse,
and sell a little cheaper.
JOHN RUSKIN

99

Those who invented the law of supply and demand
have no right to complain when this law works
against their interest.
ANWAR SADAT

66

Competition brings out the best in products
and the worst in people.
DAVID SARNOFF

99

A criminal is a person with predatory instincts who
has not sufficient captial to form a corporation.
HOWARD SCOTT

66

The big print giveth and the fine print taketh away.
J. FULTON SHEEN

99

We have to believe in free will,
we've got no choice.
ISAAC BASHEVIS SINGER

66

People of the same trade seldom meet together but
the conversation ends in a conspiracy against
the public, or in some diversion to raise prices.
ADAM SMITH

99

You never expected justice from the company,
did you? They have neither a soul to lose
nor a body to kick.
SYDNEY SMITH

66

To convert an hourly wage to an approximate
salary, double the wage and change the
decimal to a comma.
DON TICHNOR

99

A committee should consist of three men,
two of whom are absent.
HERBERT BEERBOHM TREE

66

*It's a recession when your neighbor loses his job;
it's a depression when you lose yours.*
HARRY S. TRUMAN

99

*There are two times in a man's life when he
should not speculate: when he can't afford
it and when he can.*
MARK TWAIN

66

. . . doing well that which should not be done at all.
GORE VIDAL (on commercialism)

99

*Statistics indicate that, as the result of overwork,
modern executives are dropping like flies on the
nation's golf courses.*
IRA WALLACH

66

*That which is everybody's business, is
nobody's business.*
IZAAK WALTON

99

*The trouble with the profit system has always
been that it was highly unprofitable to most people.*
E.B. WHITE

Censorship

"

Obscenity is whatever gives a judge an erection.
ANONYMOUS

"

There can be no censorship better than one's own conscience.
MICHELANGELO ANTONIONI

"

I'm all in favor of free expression provided it's kept rigidly under control.
ALAN BENNETT

"

Everybody favors free speech in the slack moments when no axes are being ground.
HEYWOOD BROUN

"

It was long accepted by the missionaries that morality was inversely proportional to the amount of clothing people wore.
ALEX CAREY

99

If one wants to see people naked one doesn't go to the theatre, one goes to a Turkish bath.
NOEL COWARD

66

Censorship is about stopping people reading or seeing what we do not want to read or see ourselves.
LORD DIPLOCK

99

Oh, I get it. It's simple. PG means the hero gets the girl, 15 means that the villain gets the girl and 18 means everybody gets the girl.
MICHAEL DOUGLAS (on UK censor ratings)

66

I dislike censorship. Like an appendix it is useless when inert and dangerous when active.
MAURICE EDELMAN

99

A stiff attitude is one of the attributes of rigor mortis.
HENRY S. HASKINS

❝

No government ought to be without censors; and where the press is free, no one ever will.
THOMAS JEFFERSON

❞

Yesterday's obscenities are today's banalities.
ARTHUR KOESTLER

❝

Murder is a crime. Describing murder is not. Sex is not crime. Describing sex is.
GERSHON LEGMAN

❞

Freedom of the press is guaranteed only to those who own one.
A.J. LIEBLING

❝

Censorship, like charity, should begin at home; but unlike charity, it should end there.
CLARE BOOTHE LUCE

❞

To forbid us anything is to make us have a mind for it.
MICHEL DE MONTAIGNE

66

A censor is a man who knows more than he thinks you ought to.
LAURENCE J. PETER

99

Obscenity is what happens to shock some elderly and ignorant magistrate.
BERTRAND RUSSELL

66

Assassination is the extreme form of censorship.
GEORGE BERNARD SHAW

99

Censorship ends in logical completeness when nobody is allowed to read any books except the books nobody reads.
GEORGE BERNARD SHAW

66

The dirtiest book of all is the expurgated book.
WALT WHITMAN

99

There is no such thing as a moral or an immoral book. Books are well written or badly written.
OSCAR WILDE

Charity

"

Altruism: the art of doing unselfish things for selfish reasons.
ANONYMOUS

"

It is more blessed to give than to receive.
THE BIBLE

"

My poor are my best patients. God pays for them.
BOERHAAVE

"

Charity is the sterilized milk of human kindness.
OLIVER HERFORD

"

As the purse is emptied the heart is filled.
VICTOR HUGO

"

That charity which longs to publish itself, ceases to be charity.
ULRICH VON HUTTON

66

*Self-sacrifice enables us to sacrifice people
without blushing.*
GEORGE BERNARD SHAW

99

*If you see anybody fallen by the wayside and
lying in the ditch, it isn't much good climbing into
the ditch and lying by his side.*
H.R.L. SHEPPARD

66

*Charity is cold in the multitude of possessions, and
the rich are covetous of their crumbs.*
CHRISTOPHER SMART

99

*The man who leaves money to charity in his will is
only giving away what no longer belongs to him.*
VOLTAIRE

66

*One can always be kind to people about whom
one cares nothing.*
OSCAR WILDE

Children

*There's only one pretty
child in the world, and
every mother has it.*
ANONYMOUS

99

*A Trick that everyone
abhors
In Little Girls is slamming
Doors.*
HILAIRE BELLOC

66

*People who say they sleep like a baby
usually don't have one.*
LEO J. BURKE

99

*Oh my son's my son till he gets him a wife,
But my daughter's my daughter all her life.*
DINAH MULOCK CRAIK

66

*There are three ways to get something done: do it
yourself, hire someone, or forbid your kids to do it.*
MONTA CRANE

99

The young always have the same problem — how to rebel and conform at the same time. They have now solved this by defying their parents and copying one another.
QUENTIN CRISP

66

You can learn many things from children. How much patience you have, for instance.
FRANKLIN P. JONES

99

Children are a great comfort in your old age — and may help you reach it faster, too.
LIONEL KAUFFMAN

66

A loud noise at one end and no sense of responsibility at the other.
RONALD KNOX (on babies)

99

The secret of dealing successfully with a child is not to be its parent.
MELL LAZARUS

66

Ask your child what he wants for dinner only if he's buying.
FRAN LEBOWITZ

99

*Insanity is hereditary; you can get
it from your children.*
SAM LEVENSON

66

*I love children, especially when they cry,
for then someone takes them away.*
NANCY MITFORD

99

*By the time the youngest children have learned
to keep the house tidy, the oldest grandchildren
are on hand to tear it to pieces.*
CHRISTOPHER MORLEY

66

*The age of a child is inversely correlated
with the size of animals it prefers.*
DESMOND MORRIS

99

*Prodigy: a child who plays the piano
when he ought to be in bed.*
J.B. MORTON

66

*A bit of talcum
Is always walcum.*
OGDEN NASH

99

*The best way to keep children at home is to
make the home environment pleasant —
and let the air out of the tires.*
DOROTHY PARKER

66

*The modern child will answer you back
before you've said anything.*
LAURENCE J. PETER

99

*You know children are growing up when they start
asking questions that have answers.*
JOHN J. PLOMP

66

*Heredity is what a man believes in until his son
begins to behave like a delinquent.*
PRESBYTERIAN LIFE

99

*Youth is a wonderful thing. What a crime
to waste it on children.*
GEORGE BERNARD SHAW

66

*There are only two things a child will
share willingly — communicable diseases
and his mother's age.*
DR. BENJAMIN SPOCK

Children: proverbs

A father maintains ten children better than ten children maintain one father.

A girl unemployed is thinking of mischief.

A little body often harbors a great soul.

A man at five may be a fool at fifteen.

A son is a son till he gets a wife, but a daughter's a daughter all the days of her life.

After a thrifty father, a prodigal son.

Chastise a good child, that it may not grow bad, and a bad one, that it may not grow worse.

Children and fools cannot lie, children and fools have merry lives.

Children and fools must not play with edged tools.

Children are certain sorrow, but uncertain joy.

Children suck the mother when they are young, and the father when they are old.

Daughters are easy to rear, but hard to marry.

He who has daughters is always a shepherd.

Kin or no kin, woe to him who has nothing.

Late children, early orphans.

Little children, little sorrows; big children, great sorrows.

Many heirs make small portions.

One kisses the child for the mother's sake, and the mother for the child's sake.

Rule youth well, and age will rule itself.

Spoilt daughters make lazy wives.

The first service a child does for his father is to make him look foolish.

Cinema

"

Several tons of dynamite are set off in this picture; none of it under the right people.
JAMES AGEE

"

An associate producer is the only guy in Hollywood who will associate with a producer.
FRED ALLEN

"

They used to shoot her through gauze. You should shoot me through linoleum.
TALLULAH BANKHEAD

"

A film should have a beginning, a middle and an end. But not necessarily in that order.
JEAN-LUC GODARD

"

A wide screen just makes a bad film twice as bad.
SAMUEL GOLDWYN

99

A good film is when the price of the dinner, the theater admission and the babysitter were worth it.
ALFRED HITCHCOCK

66

The length of a film should be directly related to the endurance of the human bladder.
ALFRED HITCHCOCK

99

Films have given me an opportunity to do things that normally you'd be locked up for, put in prison and executed for.
LEE MARVIN

66

We in this industry know that behind every successful screenwriter stands a woman. And behind her stands his wife.
GROUCHO MARX

99

The only "ism" in Hollywood is plagiarism.
DOROTHY PARKER

66

Hollywood: they know only one word of more than one syllable here, and that is "fillum."
LOUIS SHERWIN

Civilization

> **"**
> *The only thing that stops
> God sending a second
> Flood is that the first one
> was useless.*
> NICOLAS CHAMFORT
> **"**

> *The civilization of one
> epoch becomes the
> manure of the next.*
> CYRIL CONNOLLY

> **"**
> *Society is a hospital of incurables.*
> RALPH WALDO EMERSON

> **"**
> *The end of the human race will be that it will
> eventually die of civilization.*
> RALPH WALDO EMERSON

> **"**
> *In essence the Renaissance was simply the green
> end of one of civilization's hardest winters.*
> JOHN FOWLES

99

The human race never solves any of its problems. It merely outlives them.
DAVID GERROLD

66

Darwinian Man, though well-behaved at best is only a monkey shaved!
W.S. GILBERT

99

I believe I've found the missing link between animal and civilized man. It is us.
KONRAD LORENZ

66

A visitor from Mars could easily pick out the civilized nations. They have the best implements of war.
HERBERT V. PROCHNOW

99

You can't say that civilizations don't advance, for in every war they kill you in a new way.
WILL ROGERS

66

The human race has improved everything except the human race.
ADLAI STEVENSON

Clothes

66

Her hat is a creation that will never go out of style. It will look just as ridiculous year after year.
FRED ALLEN

99

An ape is an ape, a varlet's a varlet Though clothed in silk or clothed in scarlet.
ANONYMOUS

66

No one in this world needs a mink coat but a mink.
ANONYMOUS

99

Change in fashion is the tax which the industry of the poor levies on the vanity of the rich.
NICHOLAS CHAMFORT

66

You couldn't tell if she was dressed for an opera or for an operation.
IRVIN S. COBB

99

Judge not a man by his clothes, but by his wife's clothes.
THOMAS R. DEWAR

66

High heels were invented by a woman who had been kissed on the forehead.
CHRISTOPHER MORLEY

99

You'd be surprised how much it costs to look this cheap.
DOLLY PARTON

66

She wears her clothes as if they had been thrown on her with a pitchfork.
JONATHAN SWIFT

99

The only man who really needs a tail coat is a man with a hole in his trousers.
JOHN TAYLOR

66

You can say what you like about long dresses, but they cover a multitude of shins.
MAE WEST

Communication

"

Bad spellers of the world, untie!

ANONYMOUS

"

Talk is cheap because supply exceeds demand.

ANONYMOUS

"

It is all right to hold a conversation but you should let go of it now and then.

RICHARD ARMOUR

"

My father and he had one of those English friendships which begin by avoiding intimacies and eventually eliminate speech altogether.

JORGE LUIS BORGES

"

A good conversationalist is not one who remembers what was said, but says what someone wants to remember.

JOHN MASON BROWN

99

"Out of sight, out of mind," when translated into Russian (by computer), then back again into English, became "invisible maniac."
ARTHUR CALDER-MARSHALL

66

Carney's Law: There's at least a 50-50 chance that someone will print the name Craney incorrectly.
JIM CANREY

99

A man does not know what he is saying until he knows what he is not saying.
G.K. CHESTERTON

66

Nature has given to men one tongue, but two ears, that we may hear from others twice as much as we speak.
EPICTETUS

99

To work through an interpreter is like hacking one's way through a forest with a feather.
JAMES EVANS

66

I'm exhausted from not talking.
SAM GOLDWYN

99

Silence is argument carried by other means.
CHE GUEVARA

66

That man's silence is wonderful to listen to.
THOMAS HARDY

99

*Darling: the popular form of address used in
speaking to a member of the opposite sex whose
name you cannot at the moment remember.*
OLIVER HERFORD

66

*Speak clearly, if you speak at all;
Carve every word before you let it fall.*
OLIVER WENDELL HOLMES

99

*If you think before you speak, the other fellow gets
in his joke first.*
ED HOWE

66

*No man would listen to you talk if he didn't know it
was his turn next.*
ED HOWE

99

A sharp tongue is the only edged instrument that grows keener with constant use.
WASHINGTON IRVING

66

If you haven't struck oil in your first three minutes, stop boring!
GEORGE JESSEL

99

What are compliments? They are things you say to people when you don't know what else to say.
CONSTANCE JONES

66

A brilliant conversationalist is one who talks to you about yourself.
LISA KIRK

99

Shut up he explained.
RING LARDNER

66

I hate to spread rumors, but what else can one do with them?
AMANDA LEAR

99

Good communication is as stimulating as black coffee, and just as hard to sleep after.
ANNE MORROW LINDBERGH

66

If you haven't got anything nice to say about anybody, come sit next to me.
ALICE ROOSEVELT LONGWORTH

99

A speech is like a love affair. Any fool can start it, but to end it requires considerable skill.
LORD MANCROFT

66

A hypocrite is a person who — but who isn't?
DON MARQUIS

99

The real art of conversation is not only to say the right thing in the right place but to leave unsaid the wrong thing at the tempting moment.
DOROTHY NEVILL

66

Gossip is what you say about the objects of flattery when they aren't present.
P.J. O'ROURKE

99

And all who told it added something new,
And all who heard it made enlargements too.
ALEXANDER POPE (on gossip)

66

Communication is and should be hellfire and
sparks as well as sweetness and light.
AMAN VIVIAN RAKOFF

99

My father gave me these hints on speech-making:
"Be sincere . . . be brief . . . be seated."
JAMES ROOSEVELT

66

Extremists think "communication" means agreeing
with them.
LEO ROSTEN

99

Women speak two languages, one of which is
verbal.
STEVE RUBENSTEIN

66

One of the best ways to persuade others is with
your ears.
DEAN RUSK

99

Every story has three sides to it — yours, mine and the facts.
FOSTER MEHARNY RUSSELL

66

Is sloppiness in speech caused by ignorance or apathy? I don't know and I don't care.
WILLIAM SAFIRE

99

I believe in the discipline of silence and could talk for hours about it.
GEORGE BERNARD SHAW

66

I cannot learn languages; men of ordinary capacity can learn Sanskrit in less time than it takes me to buy a German dictionary.
GEORGE BERNARD SHAW

99

I learned long ago never to wrestle a pig. You get dirty, and besides, the pig likes it.
GEORGE BERNARD SHAW (on argument)

66

The trouble with her is that she lacks the power of conversation but not the power of speech.
GEORGE BERNARD SHAW

99

The cruellest lies are often told in silence.
ROBERT LOUIS STEVENSON

66

*Better to keep your mouth shut and appear stupid
than to open it and remove all doubt.*
MARK TWAIN

99

*Only presidents, editors, and people with
tapeworms have the right to use the editorial "we."*
MARK TWAIN

66

*The prime purpose of eloquence is to keep other
people from speaking.*
LOUIS VERMEIL

99

*Gossip is when you hear something you like about
someone you don't.*
EARL WILSON

66

*Gossip is the art of saying nothing in a way that
leaves practically nothing unsaid.*
WALTER WINCHELL

Computers

"

Computers are definitely more clever than humans. When's the last time six computers got together to form a committee?
ANONYMOUS

"

The computer is an inadequate substitute for human intelligence, but then so are a lot of executives.
ANONYMOUS

"

The genius of modern technology is making things to last fifty years and then making them obsolete in three.
ANONYMOUS

"

If it works, it's out of date.
STAFFORD BEER

66

Build a system that even a fool can use, and only a fool will want to use it.
ARTHUR BLOCH

99

A modern computer hovers between the obsolescent and the nonexistent.
SYDNEY BRENNER

66

Any sufficiently advanced technology is indistinguishable from magic.
ARTHUR C. CLARKE

99

The computer is down. I hope it's something serious.
STANTON DELAPLANE

66

To err is human, but to really foul things up requires a computer.
PAUL EHRLICH

99

Technological progress is like an ax in the hands of a psychopath.
ALBERT EINSTEIN

66

*A computer will not make a good manager out of a
bad manager. It makes a good manager better
faster and a bad manager worse faster.*
EDWARD M. ESBER

99

*It is only when they go wrong that machines
remind you how powerful they are.*
CLIVE JAMES

66

*The computer is down; if our world needs an
epitaph, and it may, could there be a better?*
BERNARD LEVIN

99

*Computers can figure out all kinds of
problems, except the things in the world
that just don't add up.*
JAMES MAGARY

66

*Like sex drives, card tricks, and the weather,
computers tend to be discussed in terms of
results rather than processes, which makes
them rather scary.*
MARTIN MAYER

99

*A computer cannot replace judgement, just like a
pen cannot replace literary talent. But have you
ever tried to write without a pen?*
ROBERT MCNAMARA

66

*In a few minutes a computer can make a
mistake so great that it would take many men
many months to equal it.*
MERLE L. MEACHAM

99

*Computers are useless. They can only
give you answers.*
PABLO PICASSO

66

*The real problem is not whether machines
think, but whether men do.*
B. F. SKINNER

99

*We used to have lots of questions to which
there were no answers. Now, with the computer,
there are lots of answers to which we haven't
thought up the questions.*
PETER USTINOV

Conscience and morals

❝

Conscience is a cur that will let you get past it but that you cannot keep from barking.
ANONYMOUS

❞

First secure an independent income, then practice virtue.
ANONYMOUS

❝

There is no pillow so soft as a clear conscience.
ANONYMOUS

❞

Conscience is thoroughly well-bred, and soon leaves off talking to those who do not wish to hear it.
SAMUEL BUTLER

❝

When some English moralists write about the importance of having character, they appear to mean only the importance of having a dull character.
G.K. CHESTERTON

99

The higher the buildings, the lower the morals.
NOEL COWARD

66

Moral indignation is, in most cases, two percent moral, forty-eight percent indignation, and fifty percent envy.
VITTORIO DE SICA

99

I feel bad that I don't feel worse.
MICHAEL FRAYN

66

There is perhaps no phenomenon which contains so much destructive feeling as moral indignation, which permits envy or hate to be acted out under the guise of virtue.
ERICH FROMM

99

What is moral is what you feel good after, and what is immoral is what you feel bad after.
ERNEST HEMINGWAY

66

Shame arises from the fear of man; conscience from the fear of God.
SAMUEL JOHNSON

99

*The Anglo-Saxon conscience doesn't keep you
from doing what you shouldn't; it just keeps you
from enjoying it.*
SALVADOR DE MADARIAGA

66

*Conscience is a mother-in-law whose visit
never ends.*
H.L. MENCKEN

99

*Conscience is the inner voice that warns us
somebody may be looking.*
H.L. MENCKEN

66

*Immorality is the morality of those who are
having a better time.*
H.L. MENCKEN

99

*Morality is the theory that every human act
must be either right or wrong and that ninety-nine
percent of them are wrong.*
H.L. MENCKEN

66

*He without benefit of scruples
His fun and money soon quadruples.*
OGDEN NASH

99

*What makes a boy tell his mother before his
sister does.*
LAURENCE J. PETER (on conscience)

66

*Living with a conscience is like driving a car
with the brakes on.*
BUDD SCHULBERG

99

*The nation's morals are like its teeth: the more
decayed they are the more it hurts to touch them.*
GEORGE BERNARD SHAW

66

*If your morals make you dreary, depend on it
they are wrong.*
ROBERT LEWIS STEVENSON

99

A good deed never goes unpunished.
GORE VIDAL

66

Moral indignation is jealousy with a halo.
H.G. WELLS

Courage and cowardice

66

*If you stand up to be
counted, someone will
take your seat.*
ANONYMOUS

99

*Coward: one who in a
perilous emergency
thinks with his legs.*
AMBROSE BIERCE

66

*The man that runs away
Lives to die another day.*
A.E. HOUSMAN

99

*It is better to die on your feet than to live on
your knees.*
DOLORES IBARRURI

66

*Bravery is being the only one who knows you're
afraid.*
FRANKLIN P. JONES

99

A coward is a hero with a wife, kids, and a mortgage.
MARVIN KITMAN

66

If God wanted us to be brave, why did he give us legs?
MARVIN KITMAN

99

Courage is walking naked through a cannibal village.
LEONARD LOUIS LEVINSON

66

A timid person is frightened before a danger, a coward during the time, and a courageous person afterwards.
JEAN PAUL RICHTER

99

Courage is often lack of insight, whereas cowardice in many cases in based on good information.
PETER USTINOV

66

Coward: a man in whom the instinct of self-preservation acts normally.
SULTANA ZORAYA

Courage and cowardice: proverbs

A brave man's look is worth more than a coward's sword.

A coward dies many times before his death.

A faint heart never won a fair lady.

Better pass a danger once, than always be in fear.

Brave men's wounds are seldom on their backs.

Courage is born with us, not acquired.

Cowards' weapons neither cut nor pierce.

Despair gives courage to a coward.

Fear can keep a man out of danger, but courage can support him in it.

Great things are done more through courage than through wisdom.

*He that fights and runs away, may live to
fight another day.*

He who has not courage, let him have legs.

*It is better to be a coward for one minute than
dead for the rest of your life.*

Many would be cowards if they had the courage.

*Necessity and opportunity may make a
coward brave.*

*One pair of heels is often worth two pairs
of hands.*

*Some may have been brave because they were
afraid to run away.*

The tongue talks at the head's cost.

*The weapons of war will not
arm fear.*

*Valor would fight, but
discretion would run away.*

Crime and punishment

"

*He's a good boy;
everything he steals he
brings right home to
mother.*
FRED ALLEN

"

*Organized crime in
America takes in over
forty billion dollars a year
and spends very little on
office supplies.*
WOODY ALLEN

"

*I became a policeman because I wanted to be in a
business where the customer is always wrong.*
ANONYMOUS

"

*It's not the people in prison who worry me. It's the
people who aren't.*
EARL OF ARRAN

"

*If you do big things they print your face, and if you
do little things they only print your thumbs.*
ARTHUR "BUGS" BAER

99

The Metropolitan Police Force is abbreviated to the "Met" to give more members a chance of spelling it.
MIKE BARFIELD

66

When I came back to Dublin I was courtmartialed in my absence and sentenced to death in my absence, so I said they could shoot me in my absence.
BRENDAN BEHAN

99

Prisons don't rehabilitate, they don't punish, they don't protect, so what the hell do they do?
JERRY BROWN

66

Getting caught is the mother of invention.
ROBERT BYRNE

99

When I see the Ten Most Wanted lists . . . I always have this thought: If we'd made them feel wanted earlier, they wouldn't be wanted now.
EDDIE CANTOR

66

I've been accused of every death except the casualty list of the World War.
AL CAPONE

99

You can get much farther with a kind word and a gun than you can with a kind word alone.
AL CAPONE

66

Thieves respect property. They merely wish the property to become their property that they may more perfectly respect it.
G.K. CHESTERTON

99

There is never enough time, unless you're serving it.
MALCOLM FORBES

66

Are you going to come quietly or do I have to use earplugs?
THE GOON SHOW

99

It is fairly obvious that those who are in favor of the death penalty have more affinity with assassins than those who are not.
RÉMY DE GOURMONT

66

Every once in a while some feller without a single bad habit gets caught.
KIN HUBBARD

99

I don't worry about crime in the streets; it's the sidewalks I stay off of.
JOHNSON LETELLIER

66

You are remembered for the rules you break.
DOUGLAS MACARTHUR

99

Policemen are numbered in case they get lost.
SPIKE MILLIGAN

66

A kleptomaniac is a person who helps himself because he can't help himself.
HENRY MORGAN

99

Clue: what the police find when they fail to arrest a criminal.
J.B. MORTON

66

*Never raise your hand to your children — it leaves
your mid-section unprotected.*
ROBERT ORBEN

99

*It's strange that men should take up crime when
there are so many legal ways to be dishonest.*
LAURENCE J. PETER

66

*I believe that people would be alive today if there
were a death penalty.*
NANCY REAGAN

99

*Crime is a logical extension of the sort of behavior
that is often considered perfectly respectable in
legitimate business.*
ROBERT RICE

66

*Most people fancy themselves innocent of those
crimes of which they cannot be convicted.*
SENECA

99

*The faults of the burglar are the qualities of
the financier.*
GEORGE BERNARD SHAW

❝

Should vice expect to 'scape rebuke
Because its owner is a duke?
JONATHAN SWIFT

❞

I'm all for bringing back the birch, but only
between consenting adults.
GORE VIDAL

❝

Fear succeeds crime — it is its punishment.
VOLTAIRE

❞

Murder is always a mistake — one should never do
anything one cannot talk about after dinner.
OSCAR WILDE

❝

The vilest deeds like poison weeds
Bloom well in prison-air:
It is only what is good in Man
That wastes and withers there.
OSCAR WILDE

❞

It's better to be wanted for murder than not to be
wanted at all.
MARTY WINCH

Critics

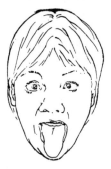

66

Critics are like eunuchs in a harem: they know how it's done, they've seen it done every day, but they're unable to do it themselves.
BRENDAN BEHAN

99

Critic: a person who boasts himself hard to please because nobody tries to please him.
AMBROSE BIERCE

66

To many people dramatic criticism must be like trying to tattoo soap bubbles.
JOHN MASON BROWN

99

In judging others, folks will work overtime for no pay.
CHARLES EDWIN CARRUTHERS

"

They who write ill and they who durst not write,
Turn critics out of mere revenge and spite.
JOHN DRYDEN

"

Taking to pieces is the trade of those
who cannot construct.
RALPH WALDO EMERSON

"

Asking a working writer what he thinks
about critics is like asking a lamppost how it
feels about dogs.
CHRISTOPHER HAMPTON

"

What is a modern poet's fate?
To write his thoughts upon a slate;
The critic spits on what is done,
Gives it a wipe — and all is gone.
THOMAS HOOD

"

A fly, Sir, may sting a stately horse and make
him wince; but one is but an insect, and the other
is a horse still.
SAMUEL JOHNSON

99

Nature fits all her children with something to do;
He who would write and can't write,
can surely review.
JAMES RUSSELL LOWELL

66

Criticism is prejudice made plausible.
H.L. MENCKEN

99

The lot of critics is to be remembered by
what they failed to understand.
GEORGE MOORE

66

A critic is a gong at a railroad crossing clanging
loudly and vainly as the train goes by.
CHRISTOPHER MORLEY

99

Insects sting, not from malice, but because they
want to live. It is the same with critics — they
desire our blood, not our pain.
FRIEDRICH W. NIETZSCHE

66

A critic is a legless man who teaches running.
CHANNING POLLOCK

99

*Can't a critic give his opinion of an omelette
without being asked to lay an egg?*
CLAYTON RAWSON

66

*I am sitting in the smallest room in my house.
I have your review in front of me. Soon it
will be behind me.*
MAX REGER

99

*When a book and a head come into contact and
one of them sounds hollow, is it always the book?*
ARTHUR SCHOPENHAUER

66

*A drama critic is a man who
leaves no turn unstoned.*
GEORGE BERNARD SHAW

99

*Reviewing has one advantage over suicide:
in suicide you take it out on yourself; in
reviewing you take it out on other people.*
GEORGE BERNARD SHAW

66

*A critic is a man who knows the way
but can't drive the car.*
KENNETH TYNAN

Cynicism

> **❝**
> *The cynic is one who never sees a good quality in a man, and never fails to see a bad one.*
> HENRY WARD BEECHER

> **❞**
> *Cynic: a blackguard whose faulty vision sees things as they are, not as they ought to be.*
> AMBROSE BIERCE

> **❝**
> *A cynic is just a man who found out when he was about ten that here wasn't any Santa Claus, and he's still upset.*
> JAMES GOULD COZZENS

> **❞**
> *A cynic is not merely one who reads bitter lessons from the past, he is one who is prematurely disappointed in the future.*
> SYDNEY J. HARRIS

> **❝**
> *Cynicism is an unpleasant way of saying the truth.*
> LILLIAN HELLMAN

99

God is love, but get it in writing.
GYPSY ROSE LEE

66

*Cynicism — the intellectual cripple's substitute
for intelligence.*
RUSSELL LYNES

99

*A cynic is a man who, when he smells flowers,
looks around for a coffin.*
H.L. MENCKEN

66

Cynicism is intellectual dandyism.
GEORGE MEREDITH

99

*The power of accurate observation is commonly
called cynicism by those who have not got it.*
GEORGE BERNARD SHAW

66

Cynicism is humor in ill health.
H.G. WELLS

99

*What is a cynic? A man who knows the price of
everything and the value of nothing.*
OSCAR WILDE

Death

> *I don't believe in an afterlife although I'm bringing a change of underwear.*
> WOODY ALLEN

> *I don't want to achieve immortality through my work . . . I want to achieve it through not dying.*
> WOODY ALLEN

> *It's not that I'm afraid of death, I just don't want to be there when it happens.*
> WOODY ALLEN

> *As soon as a man is born he begins to die.*
> ANONYMOUS

> *Death is life's answer to the question "Why?"*
> ANONYMOUS

99

Death is nature's way of telling you to slow down.
ANONYMOUS

66

*Death is the greatest kick of all. That's
why they save it till last.*
ANONYMOUS

99

*It is better to be a coward for a minute
than dead for the rest of your life.*
ANONYMOUS

66

Never speak ill of the dead.
ANONYMOUS

99

Nothing is certain but death and taxes.
ANONYMOUS

66

*Regret to inform you, the hand that rocked
the cradle kicked the bucket.*
ANONYMOUS

99

*The old man has his death before his eyes;
the young man behind his back.*
ANONYMOUS

66

There will be sleeping enough in the grave.
ANONYMOUS

99

*Funeral: a pageant whereby we attest our respect
for the dead by enriching the undertaker.*
AMBROSE BIERCE

66

*The fence around a cemetery is foolish, for
those inside can't get out and those outside
don't want to get in.*
ARTHUR BRISBANE

99

It costs a lot of money to die comfortably.
SAMUEL BUTLER

66

*The only thing wrong with immortality is
that it tends to go on forever.*
HERB CAEN

99

*For three days after death hair and fingernails
continue to grow but phone calls taper off.*
JOHNNY CARSON

66

I know a man who gave up smoking, drinking, sex, and rich food. He was healthy right up to the time he killed himself.
JOHNNY CARSON

99

There are many who dare not kill themselves for fear of what the neighbors will say.
CYRIL CONNOLLY

66

Death is what makes life an event.
FRANCIS FORD COPPOLA

99

The graveyards are full of indispensable men.
CHARLES DE GAULLE

66

Try not to take life too seriously. You're not going to get out of it alive anyway.
CARL DOUGLAS

99

Millions long for immortality who do not know what to do with themselves on a rainy Sunday afternoon.
SUSAN ERTZ

66

*Why fear death? It is the most
beautiful adventure in life.*
CHARLES FROHMAN

99

*I often wonder how I'm going to die. You
don't want to embarrass friends.*
CARY GRANT

66

Once you're dead, you're made for life.
JIMI HENDRIX

99

*Now I am about to take my last voyage,
a great leap in the dark.*
THOMAS HOBBES

66

*There are more dead people than living,
and their numbers are increasing.*
EUGENE IONESCO

99

*We are but tenants on this earth, and shortly
the great Landlord will give us notice
that our lease has expired.*
JOSEPH JEFFERSON

66

Depend upon it, Sir, when a man knows he is to be hanged in a fortnight, it concentrates his mind wonderfully.
SAMUEL JOHNSON

99

It matters not how a man dies, but how he lives.
SAMUEL JOHNSON

66

Everybody wants to go to heaven, but nobody wants to die.
JOE LOUIS

99

The living are just the dead on holiday.
MAURICE MAETERLINCK

66

Death is psychosomatic.
CHARLES MANSON

99

If death did not exist . . . it would be necessary to invent it.
J.B. MILHAUD

❝

*Death and taxes and childbirth! There's never
any convenient time for any of them.*
MARGARET MITCHELL

❞

*Those who welcome death have only
tried it from the ears up.*
WILSON MIZNER

❝

One dies only once, and it's for such a long time!
MOLIÈRE

❞

*Defeat is worse than death because
you have to live with defeat.*
BILL MUSSELMAN

❝

It's all the same in the end.
TITUS OATES

❞

Whom the gods favor die young.
PLAUTUS

❝

*Most people would sooner die than think;
in fact, they do so.*
BERTRAND RUSSELL

66

*There is no cure for death, save
to enjoy the interval.*
GEORGE SANTAYANA

99

*After your death you will be what you
were before your birth.*
ARTHUR SCHOPENHAUER

66

*Is death the last sleep?
No, it is the final awakening.*
SIR WALTER SCOTT

99

*Since we have to speak well of the dead,
let's knock them while they're alive.*
JOHN SLOAN

66

The report of my death was an exaggeration.
MARK TWAIN

99

I am dying beyond my means.
OSCAR WILDE

Death: proverbs

A young physician fattens the churchyard.

Dead men tell no tales.

Death alone can kill hope.

Death carries a fat tsar on his shoulders as easily as a lean beggar.

Death pays all debts.

Dying is as natural as living.

Every door may be shut except death's door.

Gray hairs are death's blossoms.

Men fear death as children fear to go in the dark.

Men know where they were born, not where they shall die.

Nothing is certain except death and taxes.

On the turf all men are equal — and under it.

The blunders of physicians are covered by the earth.

The dead open the eyes of the living.

The first breath is the beginning of death.

The old man has death before his eyes; the young man behind his back.

The rich widow's tears soon dry.

There is but one way to enter this life, but the gates of death are without number.

Time goes, death comes.

Until death there is no knowing what may befall.

Until hell is full no lawyer will ever be saved.

Virtue never dies.

Diplomacy

66

When a diplomat says yes he means perhaps; when he says perhaps he means no; when he says no he is no diplomat.
ANONYMOUS

99

Diplomat: a person who can be disarming even though his country isn't.
SIDNEY BRODY

66

A diplomat is a man who always remembers a woman's birthday but never remembers her age.
ROBERT FROST

99

Diplomacy is to do and say the nastiest thing in the nicest way.
ISAAC GOLDBERG

66

A diplomat is a fellow that lets you do all the talking while he gets what he wants.
KIN HUBBARD

99

A real diplomat is one who can cut his neighbor's throat without having his neighbor notice it.
TRYGVE LIE

66

A diplomat is a person appointed to avert situations that would never occur if there were no diplomats.
GERALD F. LIEBERMAN

99

In order to be a diplomat one must speak a number of languages, including double-talk.
CAREY MCWILLIAMS

66

A diplomat's life is made up of three ingredients: protocol, Geritol, and alcohol.
ADLAI STEVENSON

99

A diplomat is a person who can tell you to go to hell in such a way that you actually look forward to the trip.
CASKIE STINNETT

66

An ambassador is an honest man sent to lie abroad for the good of his country.
HENRY WOTTON

Economics

"

*A study of economics
usually reveals that the
best time to buy anything
is last year.*
MARTY ALLEN

"

*A budget is a method of
worrying before you
spend instead of
afterward.*
ANONYMOUS

"

*In all recorded history there has not been one
economist who has had to worry about where the
next meal would come from.*
PETER DRUCKER

"

*Once economists were asked: "If you're so smart,
why ain't you rich?" Today they're asked:
"Now you've proved you ain't so smart, how
come you got so rich?"*
EDGAR R. FIEDLER

66

Economics is extremely useful as a form of employment for economists.
J.K. GALBRAITH

99

In economics, the majority is always wrong.
J.K. GALBRAITH

66

The problem of economics in Britain is very much like that of sex in the United States. Both countries have enormous difficulties in keeping it in perspective.
J.K. GALBRAITH

99

There are three kinds of economist. Those who can count and those who can't.
EDDIE GEORGE

66

Moscow is the only city where, if Marilyn Monroe walked down the street with nothing on but a pair of shoes, people would stare at her feet first.
JOHN GUNTHER

99

Having a little inflation is like being a little pregnant.
LEON HENDERSON

❝

Tax cut: the kindest cut of all.
HUBERT HUMPHREY

❞

*America . . . an economic system prouder of
the distribution of its products than of the
products themselves.*
MURRAY KEMPTON

❝

*If economists were good in business they would be
rich men, instead of experts advising rich men.*
KIRK KERKORIAN

❞

*Planned economy: where everything is included in
the plans except economy.*
CAREY MCWILLIAMS

❝

*Undermine the entire structure of society by
leaving the pay toilet door ajar so the next person
can get it free.*
TAYLOR MEAD

❞

Economy: cutting down other people's wages.
J.B. MORTON

"

*If the nation's economists were laid end to end,
they would point in all directions.*
ARTHUR H. MOTLEY

"

*An economist is an expert who will know
tomorrow why the things he predicted
yesterday didn't happen today.*
LAURENCE J. PETER

"

*If all economists were laid end to end,
they would not reach a conclusion.*
GEORGE BERNARD SHAW

"

*Give me a one-handed economist!
All my economists say: "On the one hand . . .
on the other."*
HARRY S. TRUMAN

"

*It's a recession when a neighbor loses his job;
it's a depression when you lose yours.*
HARRY S. TRUMAN

"

If you're not confused you're not paying attention.
WALL STREET WEEK

Education

66

Academic staff rather enjoy coming to a conclusion, but they don't like coming to decisions at all.
NOEL ANNAN

99

An education enables you to earn more than an educator.
ANONYMOUS

66

A professor is a man whose job is to tell students how to solve the problems of life which he himself has tried to avoid by becoming a professor.
ANONYMOUS

99

There is no crisis to which academics will not respond with a seminar.
ANONYMOUS

66

A professor is one who talks in someone else's sleep.
W.H. AUDEN

99

Education: that which discloses to the wise and disguises from the foolish their lack of understanding.
AMBROSE BIERCE

66

*If you think education is expensive —
try ignorance.*
DEREK BOK

99

Most educators would continue to lecture on navigation while the ship is going down.
JAMES H. BOREN

66

It would be a great advantage to some schoolmasters if they would steal two hours a day from their pupils, and give their own minds the benefit of the robbery.
J.F. BOYSE

99

On many American campuses the only qualification for admission was the ability actually to find the campus and then discover a parking space.
MALCOLM BRADBURY

66

Intellectuals are people who believe that ideas are of more importance than values; that is to say, their own ideas and other people's values.
GERALD BRENAN

99

You can lead a man up to the university, but you can't make him think.
FINLEY PETER DUNNE

66

I pay the schoolmaster, but 'tis the schoolboys that educate my son.
RALPH WALDO EMERSON

99

An egghead is one who stands firmly on both feet in mid air on both sides of an issue . . .
HOMER FERGUSON

66

Spoon-feeding in the long run teaches us nothing but the shape of the spoon.
E.M. FORSTER

99

Everyone gets two kinds of education: one which is provided by others, and another, much more important, which comes from yourself.
EDWARD GIBBON

66

The advantage of a classical education is that it enables you to despise the wealth which it prevents you from achieving.
RUSSELL GREEN

99

The Romans would never have had time to conquer the world if they had been obliged to learn Latin first of all.
HEINRICH HEINE

66

You can always tell a Harvard man — but you can't tell him much.
ELBERT HUBBARD

99

University degrees are a bit like adultery. You may not want to get involved in that sort of thing. But you don't want to be thought incapable.
PETER IMBERT

66

Education: the inculcation of the incomprehensible into the indifferent by the incompetent.
JOHN MAYNARD KEYNES

99

You suddenly understand something you've understood all your life, but in a new way.
DORIS LESSING (on learning)

66

If you educate a man you educate a person, but if you educate a woman you educate a family.
RUBY MANIKAN

99

The reason universities are so full of knowledge is that the students come with so much and they leave with so little.
MARSHALL MCLUHAN

66

Superior people know everything without having learned anything.
MOLIÈRE

99

For hundreds of years Britain has been brilliant at educating an elite; the problem is the other eighty percent.
CLAUS MOSER

66

The university is simply the canary in the coalmine. It is the most sensitive barometer of social change.
JAMES PERKINS

99

*A man who has never gone to school may steal
from a freight car; but if he has a university
education, he may steal the whole railroad.*
THEODORE ROOSEVELT

66

*Do you know the difference between education and
experience? Education is when you read the fine
print; experience is what you get when you don't.*
PETER SEEGER

99

*Intellectuals, like fish, often move in
schools following a leader.*
ISRAEL SHENKER

66

*Economists report that a college education
adds many thousands of dollars to a man's
lifetime income — which he then spends
sending his son to college.*
BILL VAUGHAN

99

*Anyone who has been to an English public school
will always feel comparatively at home in prison.*
EVELYN WAUGH

Egotism

> 66
>
> *The last time I saw him he was walking down Lover's Lane holding his own hand.*
> FRED ALLEN

> 99
>
> *I know I am God because when I pray to him I find I'm talking to myself.*
> PETER BARNES

> 66
>
> *Egotist: a person of low taste, more interested in himself than in me.*
> AMBROSE BIERCE

> 99
>
> *If he ever went to school without any boots it was because he was too big for them.*
> IVOR BULMER-THOMAS

> 66
>
> *The advantage of doing one's praising for oneself is that one can lay it on so thick and exactly in the right places.*
> SAMUEL BUTLER

99

He was like a cock, who thought the sun had risen to hear him crow.
GEORGE ELIOT

66

He that falls in love with himself will have no rivals.
BENJAMIN FRANKLIN

99

I am always prepared to recognise that there can be two points of view — mine, and one that is probably wrong.
JOHN GORTON

66

I'm really a very humble man. Not a day goes by that I don't thank God for my looks, my stature and my talent.
TY HARDIN

99

One nice thing about egotists: they don't talk about other people.
LUCILLE S. HARPER

66

Modesty: the gentle art of enhancing your charm by pretending not to be aware of it.
OLIVER HERFORD

99

Ego: the fallacy whereby a goose thinks he's a swan.
OSCAR LEVANT

66

There are two sides to every question: my side and the wrong side.
OSCAR LEVANT

99

What the world needs is more geniuses with humility — there are so few of us left.
OSCAR LEVANT

66

Don't talk about yourself; it will be done when you leave.
WILSON MIZNER

99

There are two kinds of egotists: those who admit it, and the rest of us.
LAURENCE J. PETER

66

The greatest magnifying glasses in the world are a man's own eyes when they look upon his own person.
ALEXANDER POPE

99

An egotist is a man who thinks that if he hadn't been born, people would have wondered why.
DAN POST

66

When a man is wrapped up in himself he makes a pretty small package.
JOHN RUSKIN

99

I have often wished I had time to cultivate modesty . . . but I am too busy thinking about myself.
EDITH SITWELL

66

I should not talk so much about myself if there were anybody else whom I knew as well.
HENRY DAVID THOREAU

99

I never loved another person the way I loved myself.
MAE WEST

66

To love oneself is the beginning of a lifelong romance.
OSCAR WILDE

Endeavor

"

*If you can keep your head
when all about you are
losing theirs, perhaps
you have misunderstood
the situation.*
ANONYMOUS

"

*Success: ninety-nine
percent perspiration, one
percent inspiration.*
ANONYMOUS

"

*What do we want? Everything.
When do we want it? Now!*
ANONYMOUS

"

*Energy and patience in business are two
indispensable elements of success.*
P.T. BARNUM

"

*The first one gets the oyster,
the second gets the shell.*
ANDREW CARNEGIE

"

Actions speak louder than words.
DALE CARNEGIE

"

A period of continuous bad luck is as improbable as always staying on the straight path of virtue. In both cases, there will eventually be a cure.
CHARLIE CHAPLIN

"

To improve is to change;
to be perfect is to change often.
WINSTON CHURCHILL

"

Cultivate what the public do not like about you, that is who you are.
JEAN COCTEAU

"

Tact in audacity is knowing just how far is too much.
JEAN COCTEAU

"

The superior man acts before speaking, and then speaks in accordance with his actions.
CONFUCIUS

99

Always be sure you're right — then go ahead.
DAVY CROCKETT

66

*Discussion is the fruit of many men,
action the fruit of one.*
CHARLES DE GAULLE

66

*Faced with a difficult situation, it's to himself
that the man of character turns.*
CHARLES DE GUALLE

99

*Man is not a creature of circumstances.
Circumstances are the creatures of men.*
BENJAMIN DISRAELI

66

*Even if the prospects seem bad, you have
to carry on. Continuing to hold back could
be even more dangerous.*
DWIGHT D. EISENHOWER

99

*These times, like all times, are very good ones, if
we but know what to do with them.*
RALPH WALDO EMERSON

66

Fortune does not favor the sensitive among us: it is the audacious, who are not afraid to say —
"The die is cast."
ERASMUS

99

When in doubt, jump!
MALCOLM FORBES

66

Never put off for tomorrow what you can do today.
BENJAMIN FRANKLIN

99

One must be something in order to do something.
JOHANN W. VON GOETHE

66

Anyone who thinks they are not a genius has no talent.
EDMOND GONCOURT

99

No one can be right all of the time, but it helps to be right most of the time.
ROBERT HALF

66

We should always be prepared for the worst.
GEORGES HATSOPOULOS

99

Never mistake motion for action.
ERNEST HEMINGWAY

66

Character equals destiny.
HERACLITUS

99

*Every adversity, every failure, and every
heartache carries with it the seed of an
equivalent or greater benefit.*
NAPOLEON HILL

66

*You will take on the nature, the habits, and the
power of thought of those with whom you associate
in a spirit of sympathy and harmony.*
NAPOLEON HILL

99

*He has half the deed done,
who has made a beginning.*
HORACE

66

*The beginning is the most
important part of the work.*
HORACE

99

Action should not be confused with haste.
LEE IACOCCA

66

And the trouble is, if you don't risk anything,
you risk even more.
ERICA JONG

99

Some luck lies in not getting what you thought you
wanted but getting what you have, which once you
have got it you may be smart enough to see is what
you would have wanted had you known.
GARRISON KEILLOR

66

It's when things are going badly that you should
build. Why wait for things to pick up, and for
everything to cost more?
RAY KROC

99

Nothing succeeds like the appearance of success.
CHRISTOPHER LASCH

66

There is no such thing as bad times, I kept telling
myself. There is no such thing as bad business.
Business is there if you go after it.
ESTÉE LAUDER

99

Business affairs are not very sensitive. They rely on everyday activities, and must be decided each day.
BARON MONTESQUIEU

66

To succeed in this world, remember these three maxims: to see is to know; to desire is to be able to; to dare is to have.
ALFRED DE MUSSET

99

In any undertaking, two-thirds depends on reason, one-third on chance. Increase the first fraction and you are faint-hearted. Increase the second and you are foolhardy.
NAPOLEON BONAPARTE

66

The ideal man is not only nourished by adversity, but goes out of his way to seek out difficulties and obstacles.
FRIEDRICH W. NIETZSCHE

99

You cannot achieve great success until you are faithful to yourself.
FRIEDRICH W. NIETZSCHE

66

Whatever deserves doing, deserves doing well.
NICOLAS POUSSIN

99

You must do the thing you think you cannot do.
ELEANOR ROOSEVELT

66

*In any financial operation, you should act
before anyone has the chance to react.*
BARON PHILIPPE DE ROTHSCHILD

99

No one knows what they can do till they try.
PUBLIUS SYRUS

66

*The man who goes alone can start today:
but he who travels with another must
wait till that other is ready.*
HENRY DAVID THOREAU

99

Action creates more fortunes than prudence.
MARQUIS DE VAUVENARGUES

66

Fortune smiles on the audacious.
VIRGIL

Errors and mistakes

66

*All sins cast long
shadows.*
ANONYMOUS

99

*Every time history repeats
itself, the price goes up.*
ANONYMOUS

66

*There is nothing wrong with making mistakes.
Just don't respond with encores.*
ANONYMOUS

99

Those who do nothing are never wrong.
THÉODORE DE BANVILLE

66

*I have made mistakes but I have never made the
mistake of claiming that I never made one.*
JAMES GORDON BENNETT

99

*The weak have one weapon: the errors of those
who think they are strong.*
GEORGES BIDAULT

66

Wise men learn by other men's mistakes,
fools by their own.
H.G. BOHN

99

Truth lies within a little and certain compass,
but error is immense.
HENRY BOLINGBROKE

66

Of all the horrid, hideous notes of woe,
Sadder than owl-songs or the midnight blast,
Is that portentous phrase, "I told you so."
LORD BYRON

99

To stumble twice against the same stone is a
proverbial disgrace.
CICERO

66

It's over, and can't be helped, and that's one
consolation, as they always say in Turkey, when
they cut the wrong man's head off.
CHARLES DICKENS

99

Errors, like straws, upon the surface flow;
He who would search for pearls must dive below.
JOHN DRYDEN

66

A clever man commits no minor blunders.
JOHANN W. VON GOETHE

99

Admitting Error clears the Score
And proves you Wiser than before.
ARTHUR GUITERMAN

66

To err is human, but when the eraser wears out
ahead of the pencil, you're overdoing it.
J. JENKINS

99

If I wasn't making mistakes,
I wasn't making decisions.
ROBERT W. JOHNSON

66

The man who makes no mistakes
does not usually make anything.
W.C. MAGEE

99

Any man whose errors take ten years to correct
is quite a man.
J. ROBERT OPPENHEIMER

66

To err is human, to forgive divine.
ALEXANDER POPE

99

By the time you reach my age, you've made plenty of mistakes if you've lived your life properly.
RONALD REAGAN

66

The follies which a man regrets the most in his life are those which he didn't commit when he had the opportunity.
HELEN ROWLAND

99

Error will slip through a crack, while truth will stick in a doorway.
H.W. SHAW

66

Nothing is so simple that it cannot be misunderstood.
FREEMAN TEAGUE, JR.

99

Mistakes. Life would be dull without them.
OSCAR WILDE

Experts

> *A professional is a person who tells you what you know already, but in a way you cannot understand.*
> ANONYMOUS

> *To spot the expert, pick the one who predicts the job will take the longest and cost the most.*
> A. BLOCH

> *An expert is a man who has made all the mistakes which can be made, in a very narrow field.*
> NIELS BOHR

> *The function of the expert is not to be more right than other people, but to be wrong for more sophisticated reasons.*
> DAVID BUTLER

66

An expert is someone who knows some of the worst mistakes that can be made in his subject, and how to avoid them.
WERNER HEISENBERG

99

One who limits himself to his chosen mode of ignorance.
ELBERT HUBBARD

66

The correct behavior for an advisor is to question everything, produce nothing, and talk at the right time.
THOMAS JEFFERSON

99

Specialist — a man who knows more and more about less and less.
WILLIAM JAMES MAYO

66

All you have to do is to be correct in your predictions three times in a row, and then you can call yourself an expert.
LAURENCE J. PETER

99

An expert is a mechanic away from home.
CHARLES E. WILSON

Fame

66

A celebrity is a person who works all his life to become known, then wears dark glasses to avoid being recognized.
FRED ALLEN

99

If you want an audience, start a fight.
ANONYMOUS

66

Fame is like a river, that beareth up things light and swollen, and drowns things weighty and solid.
FRANCIS BACON

99

Acquaintance: a person whom we know well enough to borrow from but not well enough to lend to. A degree of friendship called slight when the object is poor or obscure, and intimate when he is rich or famous.
AMBROSE BIERCE

"

A sign of a celebrity is that his name is often worth more than his services.
DANIEL J. BOORSTIN

"

The celebrity is a person who is known for his well-knownness.
DANIEL J. BOORSTIN

"

Fame, like water, bears up the lighter things, and lets the weighty sink.
PEDRO CALDERON DE LA BARCA

"

Being a star has made it possible for me to get insulted in places where the average Negro could never hope to get insulted.
SAMMY DAVIS, JR.

"

If you become a star, you don't change, everyone else does.
KIRK DOUGLAS

"

Fame is proof that the people are gullible.
RALPH WALDO EMERSON

66

You have to have a talent for having talent.
RUTH GORDON

99

Now when I bore people at a party, they think it's their fault.
HENRY KISSINGER

66

Fame is the advantage of being known by people of whom you yourself know nothing, and for whom you care as little.
STANISLAUS LESZCYNSKI

99

A good part of the fame of most celebrated men is due to the shortsightedness of their admirers.
GEORGE CHRISTOPH LICHTENBERG

66

I don't have a photograph, but you can have my footprints. They're upstairs in my socks.
GROUCHO MARX

99

A celebrity is one who is known to many persons he is glad he doesn't know.
H.L. MENCKEN

66

Just because your voice reaches halfway around the world doesn't mean you are wiser than when it reached only to the end of the bar.
EDWARD R. MURROW

99

Glory is fleeting, but obscurity is forever.
NAPOLEON BONAPARTE

66

Awards are like hemorrhoids; in the end, every asshole gets one.
FREDERICK RAPHAEL

99

If I had done everything I'm credited with, I'd be speaking to you from a laboratory jar at Harvard.
FRANK SINATRA

66

Fame lost its appeal for me when I went into a public restroom and an autograph seeker handed me a pen and paper under the stall door.
MARLO THOMAS

99

When I went to America I had two secretaries, one for autographs, the other for locks of hair. Within six months the one had died of writer's cramp, the other was completely bald.
OSCAR WILDE

Fame: proverbs

A good name is sooner lost than won.

A good name keeps its luster in the dark.

A wounded reputation is seldom cured.

Any publicity is good publicity.

Common fame is seldom to blame.

Dress up a stick and it doesn't appear to be a stick.

Fame and repute follow a man to the door.

Fame is a magnifying glass.

From fame to infamy is a beaten road.

Good fame is better than a good face.

He that is good for something is the ass of the public.

National customs are national honors.

Neither handsome enough to kill, nor ugly enough to frighten.

Reputation is often got without merit, and lost without crime.

Samson was a strong man, but he could not pay money before he had it.

The devil is not so black as he is painted.

The doctor is often more feared than the disease.

The Emperor of Germany is the king of kings, the King of Spain king of men, the King of France king of fools, the King of England king of devils.

The Jew ruins himself with Passovers, the Moor with wedding feasts, and the Christian with lawsuits.

Throw enough dirt, and some will stick.

Under a gold sheath a leaden knife.

Food

"

*I will not eat oysters.
I want my food
dead — not sick, not
wounded — dead.*
WOODY ALLEN

"

*I always eat peas with
honey
I've done it all my life,
They do taste kind of
funny,
But it keeps them on the
knife.*
ANONYMOUS

"

*There are three arts: painting, music, and
ornamental pastry-making — of which past
architecture is a subdivision.*
ANONYMOUS

"

There is no such thing as a little garlic.
ANONYMOUS

66

A gourmet who thinks of calories is like a tart who looks at her watch.
JAMES BEARD

99

A gourmet can tell from the flavor whether a woodcock's leg is the one on which the bird is accustomed to roost.
LUCIUS BEEBE

66

The so-called nouvelle cuisine usually means not enough on your plate and too much on your bill.
PAUL BOCUSE

99

A meal without wine is like a day without sunshine.
ANTHELME BRILLAT-SAVARIN

66

The egg cream is psychologically the opposite of circumcision — it pleasurably reaffirms your Jewishness.
MEL BROOKS

99

We may live without friends;
We may live without books;
But civilized man cannot live without cooks.
EDWARD BULWER-LYTTON

66

*Anybody who believes that the way to a man's
heart is through his stomach flunked geography.*
ROBERT BYRNE

99

*The soup is never hot enough if the waiter
can keep his thumb in it.*
WILLIAM COLLIER

66

Life is too short to stuff a mushroom.
SHIRLEY CONRAN

99

*Do you know what breakfast cereal is made of?
It's made of all those little curly wooden shavings
you find in pencil sharpeners!*
ROALD DAHL

66

Cheese — milk's leap toward immortality.
CLIFTON FADIMAN

99

*When I demanded of my friend what viands
he preferred,
He quoth: "A large cold bottle, and a small
hot bird!"*
EUGENE FIELD

66

*Great food is like great sex — the more you
have the more you want.*
GAIL GREENE

99

*The best number for a dinner party is two —
myself and a dam' good headwaiter.*
NUBAR GULBENKIAN

66

A gourmet is just a glutton with brains.
PHILIP W. HABERMAN, JR.

99

Eat, drink, and be merry, for tomorrow ye diet.
LEWIS C. HENRY

66

*A practical cookbook is one that
has a blank page in the back —
where you list the numbers
of the nearest delicatessens.*
THOMAS HOOD

99

*Cooking is like love — it should be entered
into with abandon, or not at all.*
HARRIET VAN HORNE

66

*A cucumber should be well sliced, and dressed
with pepper and vinegar, and then thrown out
as good for nothing.*
SAMUEL JOHNSON

99

Food is an important part of a balanced diet.
FRAN LEBOWITZ

66

*Large, naked, raw carrots are acceptable
as food only to those who live in hutches,
eagerly awaiting Easter.*
FRAN LEBOWITZ

99

*"Can I have a table near the floor?"
"Certainly, I'll have the waiter saw the legs off."*
GROUCHO MARX

66

*At a dinner party one should eat wisely but not too
well, and talk well, but not too wisely.*
W. SOMERSET MAUGHAM

99

*A fruit is a vegetable with looks and money.
Plus, if you let it rot, it turns into wine,
something Brussels sprouts never do.*
P.J. O'ROURKE

66

*I'm not going to starve to death just so
I can live a little longer.*
IRENE PETER

99

*The noblest of all dogs is the hot dog:
it feeds the hand that bites it.*
LAURENCE J. PETER

66

Never eat more than you can lift.
MISS PIGGY

99

*Another good reducing exercise consists in placing
both hands against the table and pushing back.*
ROBERT QUILLEN

66

In Mexico we have a word for sushi: bait.
JOSÉ SIMON

99

A dinner lubricates business.
LORD STOWELL

66

*Cauliflower is nothing but cabbage
with a college education.*
MARK TWAIN

Food: proverbs

A fish should swim three times: in water, in sauce, and in wine.

A greased mouth cannot say no.

A melon and a woman are hard to choose.

An apple pie without some cheese is like a kiss without a squeeze.

Eat bread at pleasure, drink wine by measure.

Eggs and oaths are easily broken.

Everything has an end — except a sausage, which has two.

Fat head, lean brains.

Flattery is sweet food for those who swallow it.

Garlic makes a man wink, drink, and stink.

Hunger finds no fault with the crockery.

Hunger looks in at the industrious man's door but dares not enter.

If you want your dinner, don't offend the cook.

It is dangerous to eat cherries with the great, because they throw the stones at your head.

Many dishes make many diseases.

Raw poultry, veal, and fish, make the churchyards fat.

Sugared words generally prove bitter.

Summer-sown corn and woman's advice turn out well once in every seven years.

The full belly is neither good for flight nor fighting.

The mouth is the executioner and the doctor of the body.

There is no such thing as a good small beer, good brown bread, or a good old woman.

Freedom and liberty

66

The effect of liberty on individuals is that they may do what they please: we ought to see what it will please them to do, before we risk congratulations.
EDMUND BURKE

99

We are in bondage to the law in order that we may be free.
CICERO

66

Liberty is always dangerous, but it is the safest thing we have.
HARRY EMERSON FOSDICK

99

If some people got their rights they would complain of being deprived of their wrongs.
OLIVER HERFORD

66

Your Constitution is all sail and no anchor.
THOMAS BABINGTON MACAULAY

99

Freedom is the right to tell people what they do not want to hear.
GEORGE ORWELL

66

Men rattle their chains to show that they are free.
LAURENCE J. PETER

99

When a corrupt official hasn't got a leg to stand on, he stands on his constitutional rights.
LAURENCE J. PETER

66

Liberty doesn't work as well in practice as it does in speeches.
WILL ROGERS

99

A free society is one where it is safe to be unpopular.
ADLAI STEVENSON

66

I disapprove of what you say, but I will defend to the death your right to say it.
VOLTAIRE

99

Liberty is the one thing you can't have unless you give it to others.
WILLIAM ALLEN WHITE

Friends and enemies

66

*Before borrowing money
from a friend decide
which you need most.*
ANONYMOUS

99

*Better a thousand
enemies outside the
home than one inside.*
ANONYMOUS

66

Prosperity makes friends and adversity tries them.
ANONYMOUS

99

What is a friend? *A single soul
dwelling in two bodies.*
ARISTOTLE

66

*A false friend is more dangerous
than an open enemy.*
FRANCIS BACON

99

*The worst solitude is to be destitute
of sincere friendship.*
FRANCIS BACON

66

*Love thy neighbor as thyself, but choose
your neighborhood.*
LOUISE BEAL

99

*A true friend is one who likes you despite
your achievements.*
ARNOLD BENNETT

66

*It is well, when judging a friend, to remember
that he is judging you with the same godlike
and superior impartiality.*
ARNOLD BENNETT

99

*While your friend holds you affectionately
by both your hands you are safe, for you
can watch both his.*
AMBROSE BIERCE

66

*It is easier to forgive an enemy than
to forgive a friend.*
WILLIAM BLAKE

99

I wish my deadly foe no worse
Than want of friends, and empty purse.
NICHOLAS BRETON

66

If you want to know who your friends are,
get yourself a jail sentence.
CHARLES BUKOWSKI

99

That's what friendship means: sharing
the prejudice of experience.
CHARLES BUKOWSKI

66

It is difficult to say who do you the most
mischief: enemies with the worst intentions
or friends with the best.
EDWARD BULWER-LYTTON

99

Yet it is better to drop thy friends, O my
daughter, than to drop thy "H"s.
C.S. CALVERLEY

66

May God defend me from my friends;
I can defend myself from my enemies.
ALBERT CAMUS

99

*The one thing your friends will never
forgive you is your happiness.*
ALBERT CAMUS

66

Don't waste a minute thinking about your enemies.
DALE CARNEGIE

99

*You can make more friends in two months
by becoming interested in other people than
you can in two years by trying to get other
people interested in you.*
DALE CARNEGIE

66

*Tell me what company thou keepest,
and I'll tell thee what thou art.*
MIGUEL DE CERVANTES

99

A friend is, as it were, a second self.
CICERO

66

Man is his own worst enemy.
CICERO

99

*When your argument has little or no
substance, abuse your opponent.*
CICERO

66

*Friendship often ends in love;
but love, in friendship — never.*
CHARLES CALEB COLTON

99

*True friendship is like sound health, the value of
it is seldom known until it be lost.*
CHARLES CALEB COLTON

66

*You shall judge a man by his foes as
well as by his friends.*
JOSEPH CONRAD

99

*Reprove a friend in secret, but
praise him before others.*
LEONARDO DA VINCI

66

*Better have rich friends who can help you than
poor friends whom you can't always help.*
MARCEL DASSAULT

99

*The best way to keep your friends is to never owe
them anything and never lend them anything.*
PAUL DE KOCK

66

Fate chooses our relatives, we choose our friends.
ABBÉ JACQUES DELILLE

99

*Love your enemies in case your friends turn
out to be a bunch of bastards.*
R.A. DICKSON

66

*We should wish to behave to our friends as we
would wish our friends to behave to us.*
DIOGENES

99

Don't jump on a man unless he's down.
FINLEY PETER DUNNE

66

*A friend is a person with whom I may be sincere.
Before him I may think aloud.*
RALPH WALDO EMERSON

99

*The only reward of virtue is virtue; the only way
to have a friend is to be one.*
RALPH WALDO EMERSON

66

*If you hear someone speaking ill of you, instead of
trying to defend yourself you should say: "He
obviously does not know me very well, since there
are so many other faults he could have mentioned."*
EPICTETUS

99

*It is not so much our friends' help that helps us as
the confident knowledge that they will help us.*
EPICURUS

66

*The best way to lose a friend is to tell him
something for his own good.*
JAMES EVERED

99

*A brother may not be a friend, but a
friend will always be a brother.*
BENJAMIN FRANKLIN

66

*There are three faithful friends — an old wife,
an old dog, and ready money.*
BENJAMIN FRANKLIN

99

Damn all my friends except six — and they can be pallbearers. If they stumble, damn them too.
STEWART GRANGER

66

We never know the true value of friends. While they live we are too sensitive of their faults; when we have lost them we only see their virtues.
JULIUS CHARLES HARE AND AUGUSTUS WILLIAM HARE

99

I like a friend the better for having faults that one can talk about.
WILLIAM HAZLETT

66

One should forgive one's enemies, but not before they are hanged.
HEINRICH HEINE

99

Instead of loving your enemies treat your friends a little better.
ED HOWE

66

Friend: one who knows all about you and loves you just the same.
ELBERT HUBBARD

99

To make an enemy, do someone a favor.
ELBERT HUBBARD

66

*The fellow that calls you "brother" usually wants
something that doesn't belong to him.*
KIN HUBBARD

99

*Friends may come and go,
but enemies accumulate.*
THOMAS JONES

66

*Forgive your enemies, but never
forget their names.*
JOHN F. KENNEDY

99

Even a paranoid can have enemies.
HENRY KISSINGER

66

*There is more shame in distrusting one's friends
than in being deceived by them.*
LA ROCHEFOUCAULD

99

I get by with a little help from my friends.
JOHN LENNON

99

He is a fine friend. He stabs you in the front.
LEONARD LOUIS LEVINSON

99

*Friendship is unnecessary, like philosophy, like art
. . . it has no survival value; rather it is one of
those things that give value to survival.*
C.S. LEWIS

99

*A friend is one who has the same
enemies you have.*
ABRAHAM LINCOLN

99

The richer your friends, the more they cost you.
ELISABETH MARBURY

99

*No one is completely unhappy at the
failure of his best friend.*
GROUCHO MARX

99

*Money couldn't buy friends but you
got a better class of enemy.*
SPIKE MILLIGAN

66

Scratch a lover and find a foe.
DOROTHY PARKER

99

If all men knew what each said of the other, there would not be four friends in the world.
BLAISE PASCAL

66

Always assume your opponent to be smarter than you.
WALTER RATHENAU

99

A friendship born of business is better than a business born of friendship.
JOHN D. ROCKEFELLER

66

I ask you to judge me by the enemies I have made.
FRANKLIN D. ROOSEVELT

99

Rich people are usually suspicious (of friends). *They're afraid that everyone either wants their time, their money, or their reputation.*
FRANÇOISE SAGAN

66

Friends are generally of the same sex, for when men and women agree, it is only in their conclusions; their reasons are always different.
GEORGE SANTAYANA

99

Friendship always benefits; love sometimes injures.
SENECA

66

You can choose your friends, but you only have one mother.
MAX SHULMAN

99

Don't tell your friends their faults; they will cure the fault and never forgive you.
LOGAN PEARSALL SMITH

66

He makes no friend who never made a foe.
ALFRED, LORD TENNYSON

99

Greater love hath no man than this, than he lay down his friends for his life.
JEREMY THORPE

❝❝

*It takes your enemy and your friend, working
together, to hurt you: the one to slander you, and
the other to bring the news to you.*
MARK TWAIN

❞❞

Every time a friend succeeds, I die a little.
GORE VIDAL

❝❝

The friendship of a great man is a gift of the gods.
VOLTAIRE

❞❞

*Nine-tenths of the people were created so you
would want to be with the other tenth.*
HORACE WALPOLE

❝❝

*Associate yourself with men of good quality if
you esteem your own reputation; for 'tis better
to be alone than in bad company.*
GEORGE WASHINGTON

❞❞

*We cherish our friends not for their ability to
amuse us, but for ours to amuse them.*
EVELYN WAUGH

66

When you are down and out something always turns up — and it is usually the noses of your friends.
ORSON WELLES

99

He's the kind of man who picks his friends — to pieces.
MAE WEST

66

I no doubt deserved my enemies, but I don't believe I deserved my friends.
WALT WHITMAN

99

A man cannot be too careful in the choice of his enemies.
OSCAR WILDE

66

He hasn't an enemy in the world, and none of his friends like him.
OSCAR WILDE

99

Friendship's the wine of life.
EDWARD YOUNG

Friends and enemies: proverbs

A friend to everybody is a friend to nobody.

An enemy does not sleep.

Better a friend's bite than an enemy's caress.

Better an open enemy than a false friend.

Better a thousand enemies outside your house than one inside.

He is a good friend that speaks well of us behind our backs.

In time of prosperity, friends will be plenty; in time of adversity, not one amongst twenty.

It is good to have friends both in heaven and hell.

Lend your money and lose a friend.

One enemy is too many; and a hundred friends too few.

One may mend a torn friendship but it soon falls in tatters.

Select your friend with a silk-gloved hand and hold him with an iron gauntlet.

The best mirror is an old friend.

The biter is sometimes bit.

The only good enemy is a dead enemy.

Trust not a new friend nor an old enemy.

When good cheer is lacking, your friends will be packing.

When neighbors quarrel, lookers-on are more apt to add fuel than water.

When we ask a favor we say, "Madam"; when we obtain it, we say what we please.

Your friend lends, and your enemy asks for payment.

Genius

> *It takes people a long time to learn the difference between talent and genius, especially ambitious young men and women.*
> LOUISA MAY ALCOTT

> *Doing easily what others find difficult is talent; doing what is impossible for talent is genius.*
> HENRI-FRÉDÉRIC AMIEL

> *The difference between genius and stupidity is that genius has its limits.*
> ANONYMOUS

> *Genius does what it must, talent does what it can.*
> EDWARD BULWER-LYTTON

> *Talent is what you possess; genius is what possesses you.*
> MALCOLM COWLEY

99

Genius is one percent inspiration and ninety-nine percent perspiration.
THOMAS EDISON

66

Results! Why, man, I have gotten a lot of results. I know several thousand things that won't work.
THOMAS EDISON

99

What the world needs is more geniuses with humility — there are so few of us left.
OSCAR LEVANT

66

The genius of Einstein leads to Hiroshima.
PABLO PICASSO

99

A genius! For thirty-seven years I've practiced fourteen hours a day, and now they call me a genius!
PABLO SARASATE

66

I have nothing to declare but my genius.
OSCAR WILDE (to a customs official)

Good and evil

66

Good men need no recommendation and bad men it wouldn't help.
ANONYMOUS

99

The good die young — because they see it's no use living if you've got to be good.
JOHN BARRYMORE

66

The only thing necessary for the triumph of evil is for good men to do nothing.
EDMUND BURKE

99

Evil comes at leisure like the disease; good comes in a hurry like the doctor.
G.K. CHESTERTON

66

If you're naturally kind, you attract a lot of people you don't like.
WILLIAM FEATHER

99

Happy were men if they understood
There is no safety but in doing good.
JOHN FOUNTAIN

66

The good should be grateful to the bad — for
providing the world with a basis for comparison.
SVEN HALLA

99

We'd all like a reputation for generosity and we'd
all like to buy it cheap.
MIGNON McLAUGHLIN

66

The only good is knowledge and the only evil
ignorance.
SOCRATES

99

No good deed ever goes unpunished.
BROOKS THOMAS

66

When choosing between two evils, I always like to
try the one I've never tried before.
MAE WEST

Happiness

❝

It isn't necessary to be rich and famous to be happy. It's only necessary to be rich.
ALAN ALDA

❞

Money never prevented anybody from being happy or unhappy.
EDDIE BARCLAY

❝

The secret of happiness is not in doing what one likes, but in liking what one has to do.
J.M. BARRIE

❞

Happiness: an agreeable sensation arising from contemplating the misery of another.
AMBROSE BIERCE

❝

Happiness doesn't depend on any external conditions, it is governed by our mental attitude.
DALE CARNEGIE

99

*Happiest are the people who give most happiness
to others.*
DENIS DIDEROT

66

*Happiness makes up in height for what it lacks in
length.*
ROBERT FROST

99

*One can bear anything, except continual
prosperity.*
JOHANN W. VON GOETHE

66

*Remember that happiness is a way of travel — not
a destination.*
ROY M. GOODMAN

99

*Happiness is like coke — something you get as a
by-product in the process of making something else.*
ALDOUS HUXLEY

66

*Money and time are the heaviest burdens in life:
and among mortals, those who are most unhappy
are the ones who have more than they need.*
SAMUEL JOHNSON

99

*When you jump for joy, beware that no one moves
the ground from beneath your feet.*
STANISLAW J. LEC

66

*Happy is the man with a wife to tell him what to do
and a secretary to do it.*
LORD MANCROFT

99

*Happiness is the interval between periods of
unhappiness.*
DON MARQUIS

66

*Happiness to a dog is what lies on the other side of
a door.*
CHARLETON OGBURN, JR.

99

*Happiness is a way station between too little and
too much.*
CHANNING POLLOCK

66

*To be without some of the things you want is an
indispensable part of happiness.*
BERTRAND RUSSELL

99

The greatest happiness you can have is knowing that you do not necessarily require happiness.
WILLIAM SAROYAN

66

Happiness is not having what you want, but wanting what you have.
HYMAN SCHACHTEL

99

We have no more right to consume happiness without producing it than to consume wealth without producing it.
GEORGE BERNARD SHAW

66

Money doesn't make those who don't have any happy.
BORIS VIAN

99

The biggest enterprise, and the only one we should take seriously, is to live happily.
VOLTAIRE

66

Happiness is no laughing matter.
RICHARD WHATELY

Happiness: proverbs

A man of gladness seldom falls into madness.

Better be happy than wise.

Call no man happy till he dies.

Great happiness, great danger.

Happiness is not a horse, you cannot harness it.

Happy is he who can take warning from the mishap of others.

Happy is she who marries the son of a dead mother.

Happy is the country which has no history.

Happy is the wooing that is not long a-doing.

He that talks much of his happiness, summons much grief.

He who laughs last, laughs longest.

Laugh before breakfast, you'll cry before supper.

Laughter is the best medicine.

Laughter makes good blood.

Nothing so good as forbidden fruit.

One day of pleasure is worth two of sorrow.

Pleasure has a sting in its tail.

Take the world as it is, not as it ought to be.

The pleasure of what we enjoy is lost by coveting more.

We are all well placed, said the cat, when she was seated on the bacon.

When one has not what one likes, one must like what one has.

When the ass is too happy he begins dancing on the ice.

History

66

*History is something
that never happened,
written by a man who
wasn't there.*
ANONYMOUS

99

*Nostalgia is a
seductive liar.*
ANONYMOUS

66

*History: an account mostly false,
of events mostly unimportant,
which are brought about by rulers,
mostly knaves, and soldiers mostly fools.*
AMBROSE BIERCE

99

*Mythology:
the body of a primitive people's beliefs,
concerning its origin, early history,
heroes, deities and so forth,
as distinguished from the true accounts
which it invents later.*
AMBROSE BIERCE

66

God cannot alter the past, but historians can.
SAMUEL BUTLER

99

*God cannot alter the past, that is why he is obliged
to connive at the existence of historians.*
SAMUEL BUTLER

66

*I am incredibly eager . . . that the history which you
are writing should give prominence to my name
and praise it frequently.*
CICERO

99

History is a vast early warning system.
NORMAN COUSINS

66

*Most of us spend too much time on the last
twenty-four hours and too little on the last
six thousand years.*
WILL DURANT

99

*In essence, the Renaissance is simply the green end
of one of civilization's hardest winters.*
JOHN FOWLES

66

History repeats itself. Historians repeat each other.
PHILIP GUEDALLA

99

*What history teaches us is that men have never
learned anything from it.*
GEORG WILHELM HEGEL

66

*Very few things happen at the right time, and the
rest do not happen at all. The conscientious
historian will correct these defects.*
HERODOTUS

99

*That men do not learn very much from the lessons
of history is the most important of all the lessons
that history has to teach.*
ALDOUS HUXLEY

66

*A historian is often only a journalist facing
backwards.*
KARL KRAUS

99

*History is the version of past events that people
have decided to agree on.*
NAPOLEON BONAPARTE

66

History: a nearly defunct field of study that is of value only to the extent that it glorifies everything previously debased, and vice versa.
BERNARD ROSENBERG

99

Those who lie on the rails of history must expect to have their legs chopped off.
RUDÉ PRAVO (Czech newspaper)

66

History is the ship carrying living memories to the future.
STEPHEN SPENDER

99

Any event, once it has occured, can be made to appear inevitable by a competant historian.
LEE SIMONSON

66

Historians are like deaf people who go on answering questions that no one has asked them.
LEO TOLSTOY

99

History started badly and has been getting steadily worse.
GEOFFREY WILLANS AND RONALD SEARLE

Home and hospitality

"

Hospitality: the virtue which induces us to feed and lodge certain persons who are in no need of food and lodging.
AMBROSE BIERCE

"

Housework can kill you if done right.
ERMA BOMBECK

"

For a single woman, preparing for company means wiping the lipstick off the milk carton.
ELAYNE BOOSLER

"

Poor Housekeeping (ten times the circulation of Good Housekeeping)
ROBERT BYRNE (on a suggested magazine title)

"

Cockroaches and socialites are the only things that can stay up all night and eat anything.
HERB CAEN

99

A man's home is his wife's castle.
ALEXANDER CHASE

66

Conran's Law of Housework — it expands to fill the time available plus half an hour.
SHIRLEY CONRAN

99

Never keep up with the Joneses. Drag them down to your level.
QUENTIN CRISP

66

Cleaning your house while your kids are still growing is like shoveling the walk before it stops snowing.
PHYLLIS DILLER

99

There is such a build-up of crud in my oven there is only room to bake a single cupcake.
PHYLLIS DILLER

66

Many a man who thinks to found a home discovers that he has merely opened a tavern for his friends.
GEORGE NORMAN DOUGLAS

99

Fish and visitors smell after three days.
BENJAMIN FRANKLIN

66

*Never give a party if you will be the most
interesting person there.*
MICKEY FRIEDMAN

99

*Some people stay longer in an hour than others do
in a month.*
WILLIAM DEAN HOWELLS

66

*The telephone is a good way to talk to people
without having to offer them a drink.*
FRAN LEBOWITZ

99

Go, and never darken my towels again.
GROUCHO MARX

66

*Cockroaches have been given a bad rap.
They don't bite, smell, or get into your booze.
Would that all houseguests were as well behaved.*
P.J. O'ROURKE

99

*Cleaning anything involves making
something else dirty, but anything can get dirty
without something else getting clean.*
LAURENCE J. PETER

66

*Is that bottle just going to sit up there or are you
going to turn it into a lamp?*
NEIL SIMON

99

*In America, you can always find a party.
In Russia, the party always finds you.*
YAKOV SMIRNOFF

66

*Mr Pritchard: I must dust the blinds and
then I must raise them.
Mrs Ogmore-Pritchard: And before you let
the sun in, mind it wipes its shoes.*
DYLAN THOMAS

99

*I've got a self-cleaning oven — I have to get up in
the night to see if it's doing it.*
VICTORIA WOOD

Hypocrisy

❝

*The teeth are smiling,
but is the heart?*
ANONYMOUS

❞

*Hypocrite: one who,
professing virtues that he
does not respect, secures
the advantage of seeming
to be what he despises.*
AMBROSE BIERCE

❝

*When you say that you agree to a thing in
principle, you mean that you have not the slightest
intention of carrying it out.*
OTTO VON BISMARCK

❞

*The wolf was sick, he vowed a monk to be —
But when he got well, a wolf once more was he.*
WALTER BOWER

❝

*Man is the only animal that can remain on friendly
terms with the victims he intends to eat until he
eats them.*
SAMUEL BUTLER

99

*Is it not possible to eat me without insisting
that I sing the praises of my devourer?*
FYODOR DOSTOEVSKY

66

*Clean your finger before you point at
my spots.*
BENJAMIN FRANKLIN

99

*We live behind our faces, while they front
for us.*
MICHAEL KORDA

66

A hypocrite is a person who . . . but who isn't?
DON MARQUIS

99

*I despise the pleasure of pleasing people
whom I despise.*
MARY WORTLEY MONTAGU

66

*I hope you have not been leading a double life,
pretending to be wicked
and being good all the time.*
OSCAR WILDE

Ideals

"

*The worst way to improve
the world is to condemn it.*
P.J. BAILEY.

"

*Idealism is fine,
but as it approaches
reality the cost
becomes prohibitive.*
WILLIAM F. BUCKLEY, JR.

"

*Idealism increases in direct proportion to one's
distance from the problem.*
JOHN GALSWORTHY

"

*Living up to ideals is like doing everyday work
with your Sunday clothes on.*
ED HOWE

"

*Do not use that foreign word "ideals."
We have that excellent word "lies."*
HENRIK IBSEN

99

Man is a dog's ideal of what God should be.
HOLBROOK JACKSON

66

An idealist is one who, on noticing that a rose smells better than a cabbage, concludes that it will also make better soup.
H.L. MENCKEN

99

The idealist is incorrigible: if he be thrown out of Heaven, he makes an ideal of his Hell.
FRIEDRICH W. NIETZSCHE

66

An idealist — that implies you aren't going to achieve something.
ARTHUR SCARGILL

99

When they come down from their ivory towers, idealists are apt to walk straight into the gutter.
LOGAN PEARSALL SMITH

66

The human ideal will be the desire to transform life into something better and grander than itself.
CHARLES WAGNER

Ideas

66

Nothing is more dangerous than an idea, when a man has only one idea.
ALAIN

99

Every time a man puts a new idea across he finds ten men who thought of it before he did — but they only thought of it.
ANONYMOUS

66

Very simple ideas lie within the reach only of complex minds.
RÉMY DE GOURMONT

99

Man's mind stretched to a new idea never goes back to its original dimensions.
OLIVER WENDELL HOLMES

66

It is better to entertain an idea than to take it home to live with you for the rest of your life.
RANDALL JARRELL

99

*An idea isn't responsible
for the people who believe in it.*
DON MARQUIS

66

*It's just as sure a recipe for failure to have the right
idea fifty years too soon as five years too late.*
J.R. PLATT

99

*A cold in the head
causes less suffering than an idea.*
JULES RENARD

66

Crank — a man with a new idea until it succeeds.
MARK TWAIN

99

*Ideas won't keep:
something must be done about them.*
ALFRED NORTH WHITEHEAD

66

*The value of an idea has nothing whatever to do
with the sincerity of the man who expresses it.*
OSCAR WILDE

Ireland and the Irish

"

Put an Irishman on the spit, and you can always get another Irishman to baste him.
ANONYMOUS

"

Realizing that they will never be a world power, the Irish have decided to be a world nuisance.
ANONYMOUS

"

*The Irish are great talkers
Persuasive and disarming,
You can say lots and lots against the Scots —
But at least they're never charming!*
GAVIN EWART

"

Irish Americans are about as Irish as Black Americans are African.
BOB GELDOF

"

*The Irish are a fair people; — they never
speak well of one another.*
SAMUEL JOHNSON

99

*Ireland has the honour of being the only
country which never persecuted Jews — because
she never let them in.*
JAMES JOYCE

66

*The problem with Ireland is that it's a country full
of genius, but with absolutely no talent.*
HUGH LEONARD

99

*The Irish don't know what they want and are
prepared to fight to the death to get it.*
SIDNEY LITTLEWOOD

66

*God is good to the Irish, but no one else is;
not even the Irish.*
AUSTIN O'MALLEY

99

*I showed my appreciation of my native land
in the usual Irish way
by getting out of it as soon as I possibly could.*
GEORGE BERNARD SHAW

Journalism

"

Doctors bury their mistakes. Lawyers hang them. But journalists put theirs on the front page.
ANONYMOUS

"

No news is good news; no journalists is even better.
NICOLAS BENTLEY

"

Journalism largely consists of saying "Lord Jones is dead" to people who never knew Lord Jones was alive.
G.K. CHESTERTON

"

Journalism is organized gossip.
EDWARD EGGLESTONE

"

It isn't what they say about you, it's what they whisper.
ERROL FLYNN

99

The man who reads nothing at all is better educated than the man who reads nothing but newspapers.
THOMAS JEFFERSON

66

Reporters are like puppets. They simply respond to the pull of the most powerful strings.
LYNDON B. JOHNSON

99

Everything you read in newspapers is absolutely true, except for that rare story of which you happen to have first-hand knowledge.
ERWIN KNOLL

66

A politician wouldn't dream of being allowed to call a columnist the things a columnist is allowed to call a politician.
MAX LERNER

99

Never argue with people who buy ink by the gallon.
TOMMY LOSORDA

"

Writing for a newspaper is like running a revolutionary war. You go into battle not when you are ready, but when action offers itself.
NORMAN MAILER

"

*SIXTY HORSES WEDGED IN A CHIMNEY
The story to fit this sensational headline
has not yet turned up.*
J.B. MORTON

"

A reporter is a man who has renounced everything in life but the world, the flesh, and the Devil.
DAVID MURRAY

"

Sure I know where the press room is — I just look for where they throw the dog meat.
MARTINA NAVRATILOVA

"

Hot lead can be almost as effective coming from a linotype as from a firearm.
JOHN O'HARA

"

Journalists belong in the gutter because that is where ruling classes throw their guilty secrets.
GERALD PRIESTLAND

66

Freedom of the press in Britain is freedom to print such of the proprietor's prejudices as the advertisers don't object to.
HANNEN SWAFFER

99

Journalism — an ability to meet the challenge of filling the space.
REBECCA WEST

66

The difference between literature and journalism is that journalism is unreadable and literature is unread.
OSCAR WILDE

99

There is much to be said in favor of modern journalism. By giving us the opinions of the uneducated, it keeps us in touch with the ignorance of the community.
OSCAR WILDE

66

Rock journalism is people who can't write interviewing people who can't talk for people who can't read.
FRANK ZAPPA

Law and lawyers

"

*Wrong must not win by
technicalities.*
AESCHYLUS

"

*I learned law so well, the
day I graduated I sued the
college, won the case, and
got my tuition back.*
FRED ALLEN

"

A judge is a lawyer who once knew a politician.
ANONYMOUS

"

*A judge knows nothing unless it has been explained
to him three times.*
ANONYMOUS

"

A lawyer and a wagon-wheel must be well greased.
ANONYMOUS

"

*Be frank and explicit with your lawyer . . . it is his
business to confuse the issue afterwards.*
ANONYMOUS

"

*It is better to be a mouse in a cat's mouth than a
man in a lawyer's hands.*
ANONYMOUS

"

*Law school is the opposite of sex.
Even when it's good it's lousy.*
ANONYMOUS

"

The best client is a scared millionaire.
ANONYMOUS

"

*The law locks up both man and woman
Who steals the goose from off the common,
But lets the great felon loose
Who steals the common from the goose.*
ANONYMOUS

"

*Two farmers each claimed to own a certain cow.
While one pulled on its head and the other pulled
on its tail, the cow was milked by a lawyer.*
ANONYMOUS

"

*I have knowingly defended a number of guilty men.
But the guilty never escape unscathed. My fees are
sufficient punishment for anyone.*
F. LEE BAILEY

66

*Lawyers are the only persons in whom ignorance
of the law is not punished.*
JEREMY BENTHAM

99

*Lawsuit: a machine which you go into as a pig
and come out of as a sausage.*
AMBROSE BIERCE

66

*Lawyer: one skilled in the circumvention of
the law.*
AMBROSE BIERCE

99

*Litigant: a person about to give up his skin
for the hope of retaining his bone.*
AMBROSE BIERCE

66

*Laws are like sausages. It's better not to see
them being made.*
OTTO VON BISMARCK

99

*The rain it raineth on the just
And also on the unjust fella;
But chiefly on the just, because
The unjust steals the just's umbrella.*
LORD BOWEN

66

*A lawyer starts life giving five hundred dollars'
worth of law for five dollars, and ends giving five
dollars' worth for five hundred dollars.*
BENJAMIN H. BREWSTER

99

Laws, like houses, lean on one another.
EDMUND BURKE

66

*A lawyer's dream of heaven — every man
reclaimed his property at the resurrection, and
each tried to recover it from all his forefathers.*
SAMUEL BUTLER

99

Agree, for the law is costly.
WILLIAM CAMDEN

66

*The lawyer's vacation is the space between the
question put to a witness and his answer!*
RUFUS CHOATE

99

*When you go into court you are putting your fate
into the hands of twelve people who weren't smart
enough to get out of jury duty.*
NORM CROSBY

66

The trouble with law is lawyers.
CLARENCE DARROW

99

This contract is so one-sided that I am surprised to find it written on both sides of the paper.
LORD EVERSHED

66

America, where, thanks to Congress, there are forty million laws to enforce ten commandments.
ANATOLE FRANCE

99

The law, in its majestic equality, forbids the rich as well as the poor to sleep under bridges, to beg in the streets, and to steal bread.
ANATOLE FRANCE

66

Under current law, it is a crime for a private citizen to lie to a government official, but not for the government official to lie to the people.
DONALD M. FRASER

99

A jury consists of twelve persons chosen to decide who has the better lawyer.
ROBERT FROST

"

A successful lawsuit is one worn by a policeman.
ROBERT FROST

"

And whether you're an honest man, or whether you're a thief, Depends on whose solicitor has given me my brief.
W.S. GILBERT

"

No poet ever interpreted nature as freely as a lawyer interprets truth.
JEAN GIRAUDOUX

"

The Lord Chief Justice of England recently said that the greater part of his judicial time was spent investigating collisions between propelled vehicles, each on its own side of the road, each sounding its horn and each stationary.
PHILIP GUEDALLA

"

Lawyers spend a great deal of time shovelling smoke.
OLIVER WENDELL HOLMES

99

*A man may as well open an oyster without a knife,
as a lawyer's mouth without a fee.*
BARTEN HOLYDAY

66

*The dispensing of injustice is always in the
right hands.*
STANISLAW J. LEC

99

*A lawyer is a learned gentleman who rescues
your estate from your enemies and keeps
it for himself.*
DAVID LODGE

66

Lawyers are men who hire their words and anger.
MARTIAL

99

*A judge is a law student who marks his own
examination papers.*
H.L. MENCKEN

66

*Courtroom: a place where Jesus Christ and
Judas Iscariot would be equals, with the betting
odds in favor of Judas.*
H.L. MENCKEN

99

The penalty for laughing in the courtroom is six months in jail. If it were not for this penalty, the jury would never hear the evidence.
H.L. MENCKEN

66

Where there's a will, there's a lawsuit.
ADDISON MIZNER AND OLIVER HERFORD

99

No brilliance is required in the law. Just common sense and relatively clean fingernails.
JOHN MORTIMER

66

In cross-examination, as in fishing, nothing is more ungainly than a fisherman pulled into the water by his catch.
LOUIS NIZER

99

Lawyers are clever enough to convince you that the Constitution is unconstitutional.
LAURENCE J. PETER

66

A lawyer is a man who helps you get what is coming to him.
LAURENCE J. PETER

99

A lawyer is a man who prevents someone else from getting your money.
LAURENCE J. PETER

66

In most law courts a man is assumed guilty until he is proven influential.
LAURENCE J. PETER

99

Law school taught me one thing: how to take two situations that are exactly the same and show how they are different.
HART POMERANTZ

66

The hungry judges soon the sentence sign,
And wretches hang that jury-men may dine.
ALEXANDER POPE

99

A man's respect for law and order exists in precise relationship to the size of his pay check.
ADAM CLAYTON POWELL

66

A lawyer with a briefcase can steal more than a hundred men with guns.
MARIO PUZO

99

Lawyers are . . . operators of the toll bridge which anyone in search of justice must pass.
JANE BRYANT QUINN

66

Lawyers earn a living trying to understand what other lawyers have written.
WILL ROGERS

99

Law is a strange thing. It makes a man swear to tell the truth, and every time he shows signs of doing so, some lawyer objects.
SOLON

66

Laws are like spiders' webs which, if anything small falls into them they ensnare it, but large things break through and escape.
SOLON

99

A jury is composed of twelve men of average ignorance.
HERBERT SPENCER

66

It ain't no sin if you crack a few laws now and then, just so long as you don't break any.
MAE WEST

Law and lawyers: proverbs

A client between his attorney and counselor is like a goose between two foxes.

A good lawyer makes a bad neighbor.

A lawyer's opinion is worthless unless paid for.

Better a lean agreement than a fat lawsuit.

Fools and the perverse fill the lawyer's purse.

Good council is no better than bad council, if it is not taken in time.

He that steals honey should beware of the sting.

He who cheats a cheat and robs a thief, earns a pardon for a hundred years.

He who would lie in court, must lie sometimes low, sometimes high.

Home is home, as the devil said when he found himself in court.

It is not enough to know how to steal, one must know also how to conceal.

Laws catch flies but let hornets go free.

Laws go where dollars please.

Lawyers and painters can soon change white to black.

Little thieves are hanged by the neck, great ones by the purse.

The judge's son gets out of every scrape.

The more laws, the more offenders.

The rich man breaks the law, and the poor man is punished.

There is no law but has a hole in it, for those who can find it out.

Virtue is in the middle, said the devil, when seated between two lawyers.

Life

66

My grandfather always said that living is like licking honey off a thorn.
LOUIS ADAMIC

99

Is life worth living? That depends on the liver.
ANONYMOUS

66

Life is a jigsaw puzzle with most of the pieces missing.
ANONYMOUS

99

Life does not begin at the moment of conception or the moment of birth. It begins when the kids leave home and the dog dies.
ANONYMOUS

66

Life is a hereditary disease.
ANONYMOUS

99

*If living conditions don't stop improving in this
country, we're going to run out of humble
beginnings for our great men.*
RUSSELL P. ASKUE

66

*Life is a hospital in which every patient is
possessed by the desire to change his bed.*
CHARLES BAUDELAIRE

99

*Life is rather like a tin of sardines — we're all of us
looking for the key.*
ALAN BENNETT

66

*It is only possible to live happily ever after on a
day to day basis.*
MARGARET BONNANO

99

*Life is a maze in which we take the wrong turning
before we have learnt to walk.*
CYRIL CONNOLLY

66

*Life is a lease imposed upon the occupant without
previous communication of the conditions in the
contract.*
GUY DELAFOREST

99

*For most men life is a search for the proper manila
envelope in which to get themselves filed.*
CLIFTON FADIMAN

66

*Life is like an onion: you peel off layer after layer
and then you find there is nothing in it.*
JAMES GIBBONS HUNEKER

99

*The trouble with life in the fast lane is that you get
to the other end in an awful hurry.*
JOHN JENSEN

66

*Life is a pill which none of us can bear to swallow
without gilding.*
SAMUEL JOHNSON

99

*Life can only be understood backwards; but it must
be lived forwards.*
SÖREN KIERKEGAARD

66

*Life is what happens to us while we are making
other plans.*
THOMAS LA MANCE

99

Life is like a sewer. What you get out of it depends on what you put into it.
TOM LEHRER

66

Life isn't all beer and skittles; few of us have touched a skittle in years.
LAURENCE J. PETER

99

There is no cure for birth and death save to enjoy the interval.
GEORGE SANTAYANA

66

I have a new philosophy. I'm only going to dread one day at a time.
CHARLES SCHULZ

99

Life is like a train. You expect delays from time to time. But not a derailment.
WILLIE STARGELL

66

Life would be infinitely happier if we could only be born at the age of eighty and gradually approach eighteen.
MARK TWAIN

Love

66

All is fair in love and war.
ANONYMOUS

99

All the world loves a lover.
ANONYMOUS

66

Love is blind; friendship closes its eyes.
ANONYMOUS

99

Love makes the world go round.
ANONYMOUS

66

Love me, love my dog.
ANONYMOUS

99

No love like the first love.
ANONYMOUS

66

The way to a man's heart is through his stomach.
ANONYMOUS

99

True love never grows old.
ANONYMOUS

66

When poverty comes in the door,
love flies out the window.
ANONYMOUS

99

Love is, above all, the gift of oneself.
JEAN ANOUILH

66

First love is a kind of vaccination that saves man
from catching the complaint a second time.
HONORÉ DE BALZAC

99

Love is the delightful interval between
meeting a beautiful girl and discovering
that she looks like a haddock.
JOHN BARRYMORE

66

What is irritating about love is that it is a crime
that requires an accomplice.
CHARLES BAUDELAIRE

99

Make love to every woman you meet. If you get five percent of your outlays it's a good investment.
ARNOLD BENNETT

66

Greater love hath no man than this, that a man lay down his life for his friends.
THE BIBLE

99

Love: a temporary insanity curable by marriage or the removal of the patient from the influences under which he incurred the disease . . . it is sometimes fatal, but more frequently to the physician than to the patient.
AMBROSE BIERCE

66

Boy meets girl, so what?
BERTOLT BRECHT

99

The ability to make love frivolously is the chief characteristic which distinguishes human beings from beasts.
HEYWOOD BROUN

"

*God is love — I dare say. But what a
mischievous devil love is.*
SAMUEL BUTLER

"

*Love, in present day society, is just the
exchange of two momentary desires and the
contact of two skins.*
NICOLAS CHAMFORT

"

*Say what you will, 'tis better to be left than
never to have been loved.*
WILLIAM CONGREVE

"

*It has been said that love robs those who have it of
their wit, and gives it to those who have none.*
DENIS DIDEROT

"

*The magic of first love is our ignorance
that it can ever end.*
BENJAMIN DISRAELI

"

*Love is the irresistible desire to
be desired irresistibly.*
LOUIS GINSBERG

❝

*In love as in sport, the amateur status
must be strictly maintained.*
ROBERT GRAVES

❞

She who has never loved has never lived.
JOHN GRAY

❝

Love is a fan club with only two fans.
ADRIAN HENRI

❞

*Love is like measles — all the worse when
it comes late in life.*
DOUGLAS WILLIAM JERROLD

❝

*Love is the wisdom of the fool and the
folly of the wise.*
SAMUEL JOHNSON

❞

*The reason that lovers never weary of each other is
that they are always talking about themselves.*
LA ROCHEFOUCAULD

❝

*He gave her a look you could have
poured on a waffle.*
RING LARDNER

99

*Tell me, George, if you had to do it all over would
you fall in love with yourself again?*
OSCAR LEVANT (to George Gershwin)

66

*Love . . . the delusion that one woman
differs from another.*
H.L. MENCKEN

99

*Four be the things I'd been better without:
Love, curiosity, freckles, and doubt.*
DOROTHY PARKER

66

*It is well to write love letters. There are certain
things it is not easy to ask your mistress for face
to face, like money, for instance.*
HENRI DE RÉGNIER

99

*Love is two minutes fifty-two seconds of squishing
noises. It shows your mind isn't clicking right.*
JOHNNY ROTTON

66

*Love as a relation between men and women
was ruined by the desire to make sure of the
legitimacy of children.*
BERTRAND RUSSELL

99

To be wise and love
Exceeds man's might.
WILLIAM SHAKESPEARE

66

There are two tragedies in life. One is to lose your
heart's desire. The other is to gain it.
GEORGE BERNARD SHAW

99

When we want to read of the deeds that are
done for love, whither do we turn?
To the murder column.
GEORGE BERNARD SHAW

66

'T is better to have loved and lost,
Than never to have loved at all.
ALFRED, LORD TENNYSON

99

O tell her, brief is life but love is long.
ALFRED, LORD TENNYSON

66

All, everything that I understand,
I understand only because of love.
LEO TOLSTOY

99

Those who have courage to love should
have courage to suffer.
ANTHONY TROLLOPE

66

I can understand companionship.
I can understand bought sex in the afternoon.
I cannot understand the love affair.
GORE VIDAL

99

It is like a cigar.
If it goes out, you can light it again,
but it never tastes quite the same.
LORD WAVELL

66

Love conquers all things — except
poverty and toothache.
MAE WEST

99

Romance should never begin with sentiment.
It should begin with science and end
with a settlement.
OSCAR WILDE

Manners and etiquette

66

Mankind is divisible into two great classes: hosts and guests.
MAX BEERBOHM

99

The English are polite by telling lies. The Americans are polite by telling the truth.
MALCOLM BRADBURY

66

Charm is a way of getting the answer yes without asking a clear question.
ALBERT CAMUS

99

Oozing charm from every pore, He oiled his way around the floor.
ALAN JAY LERNER

66

I have noticed that the people who are late are often so much jollier than the people who have to wait for them.
E.V. LUCAS

99

*At a dinner party one should eat wisely but not too
well, and talk well but not too wisely.*
W. SOMERSET MAUGHAM

66

*In some remote regions of Islam it is said, a woman
caught unveiled by a stranger will raise her skirt to
cover her face.*
RAYMOND MORTIMER

99

*Tact is the art of convincing people that they know
more than you do.*
RAYMOND MORTIMER

66

*The Japanese have perfected good manners and
made them indistinguishable from rudeness.*
PAUL THEROUX

99

*Good breeding consists of concealing how much we
think of ourselves and how little we think of the
other person.*
MARK TWAIN

66

Politeness is organized indifference.
PAUL VALÉRY

Marriage

66

I tended to place my wife under a pedestal.
WOODY ALLEN

99

A deaf husband and a blind wife are always a happy couple.
ANONYMOUS

66

Bigamy is having one husband too many. Monogamy is the same.
ANONYMOUS

99

He who marries for money earns it.
ANONYMOUS

66

It is better for a woman to marry a man who loves her than a man she loves.
ANONYMOUS

99

Love is the dawn of marriage, and marriage is the sunset of love.
ANONYMOUS

66

Marriage is the only war where one sleeps with the enemy.
ANONYMOUS

99

What's the definition of a tragedy? Marrying a man for love and then discovering that he has no money.
ANONYMOUS

66

I married beneath me — all women do.
NANCY ASTOR

99

Winston, if I were married to you I'd put poison in your coffee.
NANCY ASTOR (to Winston Churchill)

Nancy, if you were my wife, I'd drink it.
WINSTON CHURCHILL (to Nancy Astor)

66

Many a man owes his success to his first wife and his second wife to his success.
JIM BACKUS

99

A woman must be a genius to create a good husband.
HONORÉ DE BALZAC

66

*The majority of husbands remind me of an
orangutan trying to play the violin.*
HONORÉ DE BALZAC

99

*My wife was too beautiful for words —
but not for arguments.*
JOHN BARRYMORE

66

*To me, marriage essentially is a contract,
and there are so many loopholes in it.*
WARREN BEATTY

99

*Bride: a woman with a fine prospect
of happiness behind her.*
AMBROSE BIERCE

66

*Marriage: the state or condition of a
community consisting of a master, a mistress,
and two slaves, making in all, two.*
AMBROSE BIERCE

99

*Love matches are formed by people who pay for
a month of honey with a life of vinegar.*
COUNTESS OF BLESSINGTON

66

*Love is an obsessive delusion that
is cured by marriage.*
DR. KARL BOWMAN

99

*We stay together, but we distrust one another. Ah,
yes . . . but isn't that a definition of marriage?*
MALCOLM BRADBURY

66

The deed involves sacrifice and risk.
MARTIN BUBER

99

*It was very good of God to let Carlyle and Mrs.
Carlyle marry one another and so make only two
people miserable instead of four.*
SAMUEL BUTLER

66

*All tragedies are finished by death;
all comedies are ended by a marriage.*
LORD BYRON

99

*The deep, deep peace of the double-bed after the
hurly-burly of the chaise longue.*
MRS. PATRICK CAMPBELL

❝

*I am not at all the sort of
person you and I took me for.*
JANE CARLYLE (to her husband)

❞

*I'm not exactly scared of marriage. It's just that,
looking around, it never works.*
JULIE CHRISTIE

❝

*My wife and I tried two or three times in the
last forty years to have breakfast together, but it
was so disagreeable we had to stop.*
WINSTON CHURCHILL

❞

*Marriage is a feast where the grace
is sometimes better than the dinner.*
CHARLES CALEB COLTON

❝

*Courtship to marriage, as a very
witty prologue to a very dull play.*
WILLIAM CONGREVE

❞

*Thus grief still treads upon the heels of pleasure,
Marry'd in hast, we may repent at leisure.*
WILLIAM CONGREVE

66

The dread of loneliness is greater than the fear of bondage, so we get married.
CYRIL CONNOLLY

99

Marriage has driven more than one man to sex.
PETER DE VRIES

66

Marriage is a romance in which the hero dies in the first chapter.
THOMAS R. DEWAR

99

There were three of us in this marriage, so it was a bit crowded.
DIANA, PRINCESS OF WALES

66

Never go to bed mad. Stay up and fight.
PHYLLIS DILLER

99

I have always thought that every woman should marry, and no man.
BENJAMIN DISRAELI

66

*There's only one way to have a happy
marriage, and as soon as I learn what it is
I'll get married again.*
CLINT EASTWOOD

99

We want playmates we own.
JULES FEIFFER

66

*Most marriages don't add two people together.
They subtract one from the other.*
IAN FLEMING

99

*People change after they're married. They die
and become so very bourgeois.*
JANE FONDA

66

*Keep thy eyes wide open before marriage,
and half shut afterward.*
THOMAS FULLER

99

*"How many husbands have you had?"
You mean apart from my own?*
ZSA ZSA GABOR

66

A man in love is incomplete until he has married. Then he's finished.
ZSA ZSA GABOR

99

He taught me housekeeping; when I divorce I keep the house.
ZSA ZSA GABOR

66

Husbands are like fires. They go out when unattended.
ZSA ZSA GABOR

99

The comfortable estate of widowhood is the only hope that keeps up a wife's spirits.
JOHN GAY

66

Love is an ideal thing, marriage a real thing; a confusion of the real with the ideal never goes unpunished.
JOHANN W. VON GOETHE

99

I . . . chose my wife, as she did her wedding gown, not for a fine glossy surface, but such qualities as would wear well.
OLIVER GOLDSMITH

66

*When a woman gets married it is like jumping into
a hole in the ice in the middle of winter; you do it
once and you remember it the rest of your days.*
MAXIM GORKY

99

*Matrimony — the high sea for which no
compass has yet been invented.*
HEINRICH HEINE

66

*The music at a wedding procession always reminds
me of the music of soldiers going into battle.*
HEINRICH HEINE

99

*It's bloody impractical: to love, honor, and obey. If
it weren't, you wouldn't have to sign a contract.*
KATHARINE HEPBURN

66

Holy deadlock.
A.P. HERBERT

99

*Monotomy: the system that allows
a man only one wife.*
OLIVER HERFORD

66

*All marriages are happy. It's the living together
afterward that causes all the trouble.*
RAYMOND HULL

99

*It is better to be the widow of a hero
than the wife of a coward.*
DOLORES IBARRURI

66

*Heaven will be no heaven to me if I
do not meet my wife there.*
ANDREW JACKSON

99

*Second marriage: the triumph
of hope over experience.*
SAMUEL JOHNSON

66

*A working girl is one who quit
her job to get married.*
E.J. KIEFER

99

*If you want to read about love and marriage
you've got to buy two separate books.*
ALAN KING

66

*Marriage is the process whereby
love ripens into vengeance.*
RUDYARD KIPLING

99

*Since the law prohibits the keeping of wild
animals and I get no enjoyment from pets,
I prefer to remain unmarried.*
KARL KRAUS

66

*Nothing to me is more distasteful than
that entire complacency and satisfaction
which beam in the countenance of
a newly-married couple.*
CHARLES LAMB

99

*The honeymoon is over when he phones
that he'll be late for supper —
and she has already left a note
that it's in the refrigerator.*
BILL LAWRENCE

66

He had lots of wives, four of them his own.
GRAHAM LORD (on Jeffery Bernard)

99

*The husband who wants a happy marriage
should learn to keep his mouth shut
and his checkbook open.*
GROUCHO MARX

66

*'Tis more blessed to give than to receive;
for example, wedding presents.*
H.L. MENCKEN

99

*Bachelors know more about women than married
men. If they did not they would be married too.*
H.L. MENCKEN

66

He marries best who puts it off until it is too late.
H.L. MENCKEN

99

*No matter how happily a woman may be married,
it always pleases her to discover that there is
a nice man who wishes she were not.*
H.L. MENCKEN

66

*The only really happy folk are married
women and single men.*
H.L. MENCKEN

99

*Husbands never become good; they
merely become proficient.*
H.L. MENCKEN

66

Marry me and you'll be farting through silk.
ROBERT MITCHUM

99

*Marriage is like a cage; one sees the birds
outside desperate to get in, and those
inside desperate to get out.*
MICHEL DE MONTAIGNE

66

*The trouble with wedlock is that there's
not enough wed and too much lock.*
CHRISTOPHER MORLEY

99

*Our marriage works because we each
carry clubs of equal weight and size.*
PAUL NEWMAN

66

*Marriage may often be a stormy lake, but celibacy
is almost always a muddy horsepond:*
THOMAS LOVE PEACOCK

99

*My wife, who, poor wretch, is troubled
with her lonely life.*
SAMUEL PEPYS

66

*Marriage is like paying an endless
visit in your worst clothes.*
J.B. PRIESTLEY

99

*Marriage is a lottery in which men stake their
liberty, and women their happiness.*
MME DE RIEUX

66

*Trust your husband, adore your husband, and get
as much as you can in your own name.*
JOAN RIVERS

99

*I'm the only man in the world whose marriage
license reads: "To whom it may concern."*
MICKEY ROONEY

66

*Never feel remorse for what you have
thought about your wife. She has thought
much worse things about you.*
JEAN ROSTAND

99

*A husband is what's left of the lover once
the nerve has been extracted.*
HELEN ROWLAND

66

Marriage: a souvenir of love.
HELEN ROWLAND

99

*When a girl marries she exchanges the attentions
of many men for the inattention of one.*
HELEN ROWLAND

66

*Marriage is the Western custom of one wife
and hardly any mistresses.*
SAKI

99

A young man married is a man that's marred.
WILLIAM SHAKESPEARE

66

*It is a woman's business to get married as
soon as possible, and a man's to keep
unmarried as long as he can.*
GEORGE BERNARD SHAW

99

Marriage is popular because it combines the maximum of temptation with the maximum of opportunity.
GEORGE BERNARD SHAW

66

'Tis safest in matrimony to begin with a little aversion.
RICHARD BRINSLEY SHERIDAN

99

My definition of marriage . . . it resembles a pair of shears, so joined that they cannot be separated; often moving in opposite directions, yet always punishing anyone who comes between them.
SYDNEY SMITH

66

The surest way to be alone is to get married.
GLORIA STEINEM

99

Marriage is a friendship recognized by the police.
ROBERT LOUIS STEVENSON

66

Why does a woman work ten years to change a man's habits and then complain that he's not the man she married?
BARBRA STREISAND

99

Marriages are made in heaven.
ALFRED, LORD TENNYSON

66

*I've married a few people I shouldn't have, but
haven't we all.*
MAMIE VAN DOREN

99

Marriage isn't a word . . . it's a sentence.
KING VIDOR

66

*He's the kind of man a woman would
have to marry to get rid of.*
MAE WEST

99

*Marriage is a great institution,
but I'm not ready for an institution.*
MAE WEST

66

*If we men married the women we deserve we
should have a very bad time of it.*
OSCAR WILDE

99

*Polygamy — how much more poetic it
is to marry one and love many.*
OSCAR WILDE

66

*The proper basis for marriage
is mutual misunderstanding.*
OSCAR WILDE

99

*The real drawback of marriage is that it makes one
unselfish. And unselfish people are colorless.*
OSCAR WILDE

66

*There is one thing worse than an absolutely
loveless marriage. A marriage in which there
is love, but on one side only.*
OSCAR WILDE

99

*Twenty years of romance make a woman look
like a ruin; but twenty years of marriage make
her look like a public building.*
OSCAR WILDE

66

*'Tis my maxim, he's a fool that marries, but he's a
greater that does not marry a fool.*
WILLIAM WYCHERLEY

Marriage: proverbs

A deaf husband and a blind wife are always a happy couple.

As the good man says, so say we, but as the good wife says, so must it be.

Better be an old man's darling than a young man's slave.

Choose a wife by your ear rather than by your eye.

Early wed, early dead.

He that marries a widow will often have a dead man's head thrown in his dish.

Honest men marry soon, wise men not at all.

Keep your eyes wide open before marriage, and half shut afterwards.

Love is a fair garden and marriage a field of nettles.

Maids want nothing but husbands, and when they have them they want everything.

Man proposes, God disposes.

Marriage halves our griefs, doubles our joys, and quadruples our expenses.

Marrying is easy, but housekeeping is hard.

Matrimony is a school in which one learns too late.

Needles and pins, needles and pins: when a man marries his trouble begins.

Never marry for money, you'll borrow it cheaper.

The first wife is matrimony, the second company, the third heresy.

Whosoever is tired of happy days, let him take a wife.

Why buy a cow when milk is so cheap?

Medicine and medics

"

A psychiatrist is a fellow who asks you a lot of expensive questions your wife asks for nothing.
JOEY ADAMS

"

Your body is just like a bar of soap. It gradually wears down, from repeated use.
RITCHIE ALLEN

"

*Physicians of the Utmost Fame
Were called at once: but when they came
They answered, as they took their Fees,
"There is no Cure for this Disease."*
HILAIRE BELLOC

"

I got the bill for my surgery. Now I know what these doctors were wearing masks for.
JAMES H. BOREN

"

Psychiatrist: a person who pulls habits out of rats.
DOUGLAS BUSH

99

*Doctors are just the same as lawyers; the only
difference is that lawyers merely rob you, whereas
doctors rob you and kill you, too.*
ANTON CHEKHOV

66

*My message to the businessmen of this country
when they go abroad on business is that there is
one thing above all they can take with them to stop
them catching AIDS, and that is the wife.*
EDWINA CURRIE

99

*The best doctor is the one you run
for and can't find.*
DENIS DIDEROT

66

*Whenever patients come to I,
I physics, bleeds, and sweats 'em;
If after that they choose to die,
What's that to me! — I letts 'em.*
THOMAS ERSKINE (on Dr. John Lettsom)

99

*Psychiatry is the art of teaching people how to
stand on their own feet while reclining on couches.*
SHANNON FIFE

66

Half the modern drugs could well be thrown out the window except that the birds might eat them.
MARTIN H. FISCHER

99

God heals, and the doctor takes the fee.
BENJAMIN FRANKLIN

66

Anybody who goes to see a psychiatrist ought to have his head examined.
SAMUEL GOLDWYN

99

The kind of doctor I want is one who, when he's not examining me, is home studying medicine.
GEORGE S. KAUFMAN

66

One of the most difficult things to contend with in a hospital is the assumption on the part of the staff that because you have lost your gall bladder you have also lost your mind.
JEAN KERR

99

Psychiatry enables us to correct our faults by confessing our parents' shortcomings.
LAURENCE J. PETER

❝

Optimistic lies have such immense therapeutic value that a doctor who cannot tell them convincingly has mistaken his profession.
GEORGE BERNARD SHAW

❞

Only do always in health what you have often promised to do when you are sick.
SIGISMUND

❝

I've already had medical attention — a dog licked me when I was on the ground.
NEIL SIMON

❞

A psychiatrist is a man who goes to the Folies-Bergère and looks at the audience.
MERVYN STOCKWOOD

❝

The art of medicine consists of amusing the patient while nature cures the disease.
VOLTAIRE

❞

A neurotic is the man who builds a castle in the air. A psychotic is the man who lives in it. And a psychiatrist is the man who collects the rent.
LORD WEBB-JOHNSTONE

Men

66

*My brain? It's my second
favorite organ.*
WOODY ALLEN

99

*A gentleman is a man who
can disagree without
being disagreeable.*
ANONYMOUS

66

*A man is never so weak as when a woman
is telling him how strong he is.*
ANONYMOUS

99

*Men fantasize about being in bed with two
women. Women fantasize about it too
because at least they'll have someone to
talk to when he falls asleep.*
ANONYMOUS

66

*My husband's mind is like a Welsh railroad —
one track and dirty.*
ANONYMOUS

99

Women have many faults, men have only two:
everything they say and everything they do.
ANONYMOUS

66

The fastest way to a man's heart is
through his chest.
ROSEANNE BARR

99

Most of us grow up to be the kind of men our
mothers warned us against.
BRENDAN BEHAN

66

Man: an animal (whose) . . . chief occupation is
extermination of other animals and his own
species, which, however, multiplies with such
insistent rapidity as to infest the whole
habitable earth and Canada.
AMBROSE BIERCE

99

I insist on believing that some men are my equals.
BRIGID BROPHY

66

Every man is as God hath made him,
and sometimes a great deal worse.
MIGUEL DE CERVANTES

99

*Imprisoned in every fat man is a thin one
wildly signaling to be let out.*
CYRIL CONNOLLY

66

Macho does not prove mucho.
ZSA ZSA GABOR

99

*Probably the only place where a man can feel
really secure is in a maximum security prison,
except for the imminent threat of release.*
GERMAINE GREER

66

*Can you imagine a world without men? No crime
and lots of happy, fat women.*
NICOLE HOLLANDER

99

*If men could get pregnant, abortion
would be a sacrament.*
FLORYNCE KENNEDY

66

*Never trust a man who combs his hair
straight from his left armpit.*
ALICE ROOSEVELT LONGWORTH

99

Men are creatures with two legs and eight hands.
JAYNE MANSFIELD

66

*American women expect to find in their husbands
a perfection that English women only hope to
find in their butlers.*
W. SOMERSET MAUGHAM

99

*Don't accept rides from strange men, and
remember that all men are strange.*
ROBIN MORGAN

66

*Behind every great man there is
a surprised woman.*
MARYON PEARSON

99

*The follies which a man regrets most in
his life are those which he didn't commit
when he had the opportunity.*
HELEN ROWLAND

66

*I like men to behave like men —
strong and childish.*
FRANÇOISE SAGAN

99

Men of few words are the best men.
WILLIAM SHAKESPEARE

66

*A man is like a phonograph with half a dozen
records. You soon get tired of them all;
and yet you have to sit at the table
whilst he reels them off to every new visitor.*
GEORGE BERNARD SHAW

99

The more I see of men, the more I like dogs.
MADAME DE STAËL

66

*God made some men big and others small.
Samuel Colt made all men equal.*
JOHN THOMPSON

99

*No man thinks there is much ado about
nothing when the ado is about himself.*
ANTHONY TROLLOPE

66

*Man — a creature made at the end of the
week's work when God was tired.*
MARK TWAIN

99

A man in the house is worth two in the street.
MAE WEST

66

*He's the kind of man a woman would have
to marry to get rid of.*
MAE WEST

99

*His mother should have thrown him
away and kept the stork.*
MAE WEST

66

I only like two kinds of men: domestic and foreign.
MAE WEST

99

The best way to hold a man is in your arms.
MAE WEST

66

*A woman may race to get a man a gift,
but it always ends in a tie.*
EARL WILSON

99

If you catch a man, throw him back.
WOMEN'S LIBERATION SLOGAN

Men: proverbs

A clever man will build a city, a clever woman will lay it low.

A man is as old as he feels, and a woman as old as she looks.

A man often kisses the hand he would gladly see cut off.

A rich man is never ugly in the eyes of a girl.

Bachelor, a peacock; betrothed, a lion; married, an ass.

Early to bed and early to rise, makes a man healthy, wealthy, and wise.

Great men have great faults.

He who says what he likes shall hear what he does not like.

Many a man labors for the day he will never live to see.

Men get wealth and women keep it.

Remember man and keep in mind, a faithful friend is hard to find.

Show me a poor man, I will show you a flatterer.

The man of your own trade is your enemy.

The man who lives alone is either a beast or an angel.

The greater the man, the greater the crimes.

The poor man wants much, the miser everything.

The wise man does not hang his knowledge on a hook.

The wise man has long ears and a short tongue.

Three things drive a man out of doors: smoke, a leaky roof, and a bad-tempered woman.

What man has made, man can destroy.

Money and wealth

66

Bankruptcy is a legal proceeding in which you put your money in your pants pocket and give your coat to your creditors.
JOEY ADAMS

99

Money is better than poverty, if only for financial reasons.
WOODY ALLEN

66

Better to be nouveau than never to have been riche at all.
ANONYMOUS

99

Enjoy money while you have it. Shrouds don't have pockets.
ANONYMOUS

"

*If the rich could hire other people to die for them,
the poor would make a wonderful living.*
ANONYMOUS

"

*Marry for money, my little sonny,
a rich man's joke is always funny.*
ANONYMOUS

"

Money begets money.
ANONYMOUS

"

*The Eiffel Tower is the Empire State Building
after taxes.*
ANONYMOUS

"

*The reason some people are stingy is also the
reason they are rich.*
ANONYMOUS

"

The wages of sin are unreported.
ANONYMOUS

66

To get back on your feet, miss two car payments.
ANONYMOUS

99

When money speaks the truth is silent.
ANONYMOUS

66

Where gold speaks every tongue is silent.
ANONYMOUS

99

*Whoever said money can't buy happiness didn't
know where to shop.*
ANONYMOUS

66

*Why is there so much month left at the end of the
money?*
ANONYMOUS

99

Money makes the man.
ARISTODEMUS

66

*That money talks I'll not deny,
I heard it once: It said, "Goodbye."*
RICHARD ARMOUR

99

Money is something you got to make in case you don't die.
MAX ASNAS

66

A man who has a million dollars is as well off as if he were rich.
NANCY ASTOR

99

Money is like muck, not good except it be spread.
FRANCIS BACON

66

Riches are a good handmaid, but the worst mistress.
FRANCIS BACON

99

Anyone who has ever struggled with poverty knows how extremely expensive it is to be poor.
JAMES BALDWIN

66

Money, it turned out, was exactly like sex, you thought of nothing else if you didn't have it and thought of other things if you did.
JAMES BALDWIN

99

Behind every great fortune there is a crime.
HONORÉ DE BALZAC

66

*If you would know what the Lord God thinks of
money, you have only to look at those to whom
He gives it.*
MAURICE BARING

99

Every crowd has a silver lining.
P.T. BARNUM

66

*Buy old masters. They bring better prices than
young mistresses.*
LORD BEAVERBROOK

99

*Money speaks sense in a language all nations
understand.*
APHRA BEHN

66

*A feast is made for laughter, and wine maketh
merry: but money answereth all things.*
THE BIBLE

99

It is easier for a camel to go through the eye of a needle, than for a rich man to enter into the kingdom of God.
THE BIBLE

66

The love of money is the root of all evil.
THE BIBLE

99

Why does a slight tax increase cost you two hundred dollars and a substantial tax cut save you thirty cents?
PEG BRACKEN

66

We were so poor, my mother couldn't afford to have me. The lady next door gave birth to me.
MEL BROOKS

99

People who have made money always want to look like people who have inherited money.
MARIO BUATTA

66

A fool and his money are soon parted.
GEORGE BUCHANAN

99

If we command our wealth,
we shall be rich and free;
if our wealth commands us,
we are poor indeed.
EDMUND BURKE

66

Penny wise, pound foolish.
ROBERT BURTON

99

It has been said that the love of money is the root of
all evil. The want of money is so quite as truly.
SAMUEL BUTLER

66

Poor people always lean forward when they speak
because they want people to listen to them. Rich
people can sit back.
MICHAEL CAINE

99

It is a kind of spiritual snobbery that makes people
think that they can be happy without money.
ALBERT CAMUS

66

There are people who have money and people who
are rich.
COCO CHANEL

99

*The rich man may never get into heaven, but the
pauper is already serving his term in hell.*
ALEXANDER CHASE

66

*To be clever enough to get a great deal of money,
one must be stupid enough to want it.*
G.K. CHESTERTON

99

*I was seven years old before I used a toilet that
flushed. We had the kind of toilet where when it
was full, you covered it over and dug a new one.*
TOMMY CHONG

66

*Where large sums of money are concerned, it is
advisable to trust nobody.*
AGATHA CHRISTIE

99

*Gentility is what is left over from rich ancestors
after the money is gone.*
JOHN CIARDI

66

*I'm living so far beyond my income that we may
almost be said to be living apart.*
E.E. CUMMINGS

99

The major inconvenience about being poor is that it takes up all your time.
WILLIAM DE KOONING

66

How much money did you make last year? Mail it in.
STANTON DELAPLANE (on a suggestion for a simplified tax form)

99

Annual income twenty pounds, annual expenditure nineteen pounds nineteen shillings and six pence, result happiness. Annual income twenty pounds, annual expenditure twenty pounds ought and sixpence, result misery.
CHARLES DICKENS

66

A billion here, a billion there — pretty soon it adds up to real money.
EVERETT DIRKSEN

99

What's worth doing is worth doing for money.
JOSEPH DONOHUE

66

All heiresses are beautiful.
JOHN DRYDEN

99

Money will say more in one moment than the most eloquent lover can in years.
HENRY FIELDING

66

My problem lies in reconciling my gross habits with my net income.
ERROL FLYNN

99

People who say that money isn't everything in life are usually broke.
MALCOLM FORBES

66

Creditors have better memories than debtors.
BENJAMIN FRANKLIN

99

If you would know the value of money, try to borrow some.
BENJAMIN FRANKLIN

66

Nothing but money is sweeter than honey.
BENJAMIN FRANKLIN

99

Money differs from an automobile, a mistress or cancer in being equally important to those who have it and those who do not.
J.K. GALBRAITH

66

Wealth is not without its advantages.
J.K. GALBRAITH

99

If you can actually count your money then you are not really a rich man.
J. PAUL GETTY

66

The meek shall inherit the earth but not its mineral rights.
J. PAUL GETTY

99

It is no disgrace to be poor, but it might as well be.
JIM GRUE

66

The best way to help the poor is not to become one of them.
LAING HANCOCK

99

*Save a little money each month and at the end of
the year you'll be surprised at how little you have.*
ERNEST HASKINS

66

*A bank is a place that will lend you money if you
can prove that you don't need it.*
BOB HOPE

99

*Make money: make it honestly if possible; if not,
make it by any means.*
HORACE

66

*A man is usually more careful of his money than he
is of his principles.*
ED HOWE

99

*Inherited wealth is a big handicap to happiness. It
is as certain death to ambition as cocaine is to
morality.*
ED HOWE

66

*The safest way to double your money is to fold it
over once and put it in your pocket.*
KIN HUBBARD

99

I don't think you can spend yourself rich.
GEORGE HUMPHREY

66

Money no longer talks. It just goes without saying.
GEORGE HUMPHREY

99

*Man must choose whether to be rich in things or in
the freedom to use them.*
IVAN ILLICH

66

*Men are more often bribed by their loyalties and
ambitions than money.*
ROBERT JACKSON

99

*Money, and not morality, is the principle of
commercial nations.*
THOMAS JEFFERSON

66

It is better to live rich than to die rich.
SAMUEL JOHNSON

99

*There are few ways in which a man can be more
innocently employed than in getting money.*
SAMUEL JOHNSON

66

*I never been in no situation where havin' money
made it any worse.*
CLINTON JONES

99

*One of the benefits of inflation is that kids can no
longer get sick on a nickel's worth of candy.*
JOURNEYMAN BARBER MAGAZINE

66

The love of money grows as the money itself grows.
JUVENAL

99

*Great moments in science: Einstein discovers that
time is actually money.*
GARY LARSON

66

*For I don't care too much for money,
For money can't buy me love.*
JOHN LENNON (with PAUL McCARTNEY)

99

*The rich are different from you and me because
they have more credit.*
JOHN LEONARD

❝

There's only one thing money won't buy,
and that's poverty.
JOE E. LEWIS

❞

How do you make a million? You start with
$900,000.
STEPHEN LEWIS

❝

I don't believe in principal
But oh, I do in interest.
JAMES RUSSELL LOWELL

❞

Take care of the pence,
and the pounds will take care of themselves.
WILLIAM LOWNDES

❝

The richer your friends,
the more they will cost you.
ELIZABETH MARBURY

❞

I have enough money to last me the rest of my life,
unless I buy something.
JACKIE MASON

66

Gentlemen prefer bonds.
ANDREW MELLON

99

*The chief value of money lies in the fact that one
lives in a world in which it is overestimated.*
H.L. MENCKEN

66

*Money can't buy friends,
but you can get a better class of enemy.*
SPIKE MILLIGAN

99

*For every person who dreams of making fifty
thousand dollars, a hundred people dream of being
left fifty thousand dollars.*
A.A. MILNE

66

I am rich beyond the dreams of avarice.
EDWARD MOORE

99

*About money and sex it is impossible to be truthful
ever, one's ego is too involved.*
MALCOLM MUGGERIDGE

66

The buck stops with the guy who signs the checks.
RUPERT MURDOCH

99

Certainly there are things in life that money can't buy, but it's very funny — did you ever try buying them without money?
OGDEN NASH

66

He without benefit of scruples
His fun and money soon quadruples
OGDEN NASH

99

Some people's money is merited
And other people's is inherited.
OGDEN NASH

66

Money is a sixth sense which makes it possible for us to enjoy the other five.
RICHARD NEY

99

Every morning I get up and look through the Forbes list of the richest people in America. If I'm not in there, I go to work.
ROBERT ORBEN

66

Add little to little and there will be a great heap.
OVID

99

*The two most beautiful words in the English
language are "check enclosed."*
DOROTHY PARKER

66

*There is no stronger craving in the world
than that of the rich for titles,
except that of the titled for riches.*
HESKETH PEARSON

99

*Few of us ever test our powers of deduction,
except when filling out an income tax form.*
LAURENCE J. PETER

66

*Money can't buy you happiness,
but it can buy you the kind of misery you prefer.*
LAURENCE J. PETER

99

*The only problems money can solve
are money problems.*
LAURENCE J. PETER

66

*Money will come
when you are doing the right thing.*
MICHAEL PHILIPS

99

*I'd like to live like a poor man,
but with a lot of money.*
PABLO PICASSO

66

*You must spend money,
if you wish to make money.*
PLAUTUS

99

*Not having to worry about money
is almost like not having to worry about dying.*
MARIO PUZO

66

*Money is good for bribing yourself through the
inconveniences of life.*
GOTTFRIED REINHARDT

99

Owning capital is not a productive activity.
JOAN ROBINSON

66

*I believe that the power to make money is a gift
from God.*
JOHN D. ROCKEFELLER

99

*I made a resolution to let my money work
instead of me!*
JOHN D. ROCKEFELLER

66

*The income tax system has made liars out of more
Americans than golf.*
WILL ROGERS

99

*Never invest your money in anything that
eats or needs repairing.*
BILLY ROSE

66

*Money is the seed of money,
and the first guinea is sometimes more difficult to
acquire than the second million.*
JEAN JACQUES ROUSSEAU

99

*"My boy," he says, "always try to rub up against
money, for if you rub up against money long
enough, some of it may rub off on you."*
DAMON RUNYON

66

*It is preoccupation with possession,
more than anything else,
that prevents men from living freely and nobly.*
BERTRAND RUSSELL

99

*The rich have a passion for bargains
as lively as it is pointless.*
FRANÇOISE SAGAN

66

*Wealth is like sea-water; the more we drink,
the thirstier we become.*
ARTHUR SCHOPENHAUER

99

There must be more to life than having everything.
MAURICE SENDAK

66

A great fortune is a great slavery.
SENECA

99

*Make money and the whole nation will conspire to
call you a gentleman.*
GEORGE BERNARD SHAW

❝

Money brings some happiness. But after a certain point it just brings more money.
NEIL SIMON

❞

The wretchedness of being rich is that you live with rich people.
LOGAN PEARSALL SMITH

❝

*Let all the learned say what they can,
'Tis ready money makes the man.*
WILLIAM SOMERVILLE

❞

The best things in life are free, but you can leave them to the birds and bees — I want money (that's what I want).
SPICE GIRLS (ORIGINALLY BENNY, GORDY, AND BRADFORD)

❝

Money is always there, but the pockets change.
GERTRUDE STEIN

❞

Nothing makes a man and wife feel closer, these days, than a joint tax return.
GIL STERN

❝

*No one would remember the Good Samaritan
if he'd only had good intentions.
He had money as well.*
MARGARET THATCHER

❞

*Pennies do not come from heaven.
They have to be earned here on earth.*
MARGARET THATCHER

❝

*There were times my pants were so thin I could sit
on a dime and tell if it was heads or tails.*
SPENCER TRACY

❞

*I have been poor and I have been rich.
Rich is better.*
SOPHIE TUCKER

❝

*There are two times in a man's life when he
should not speculate: when he can't afford it,
and when he can.*
MARK TWAIN

❞

*What is the difference between a taxidermist and a
tax collector? The taxidermist only takes your skin.*
MARK TWAIN

66

Money won't buy happiness,
but it will pay the salaries of a large research staff
to study the problem.
BILL VAUGHAN

99

When it is a question of money,
everybody is of the same religion.
VOLTAIRE

66

Let us all be happy and live within our means,
even if we have to borrow the money to do it with.
ARTEMUS WARD

99

It is not a custom with me to keep money to look at.
GEORGE WASHINGTON

66

The easiest way for your children to learn about
money is for you not to have any.
KATHERINE WHITEHORN

99

You can be young without money but you can't be
old without it.
TENNESSEE WILLIAMS

Music

66

The opera is like a husband with a foreign title — expensive to support, hard to understand, and therefore a supreme social challenge.
CLEVELAND AMORY

99

Modern music, I don't like it. I stood in some once.
ANONYMOUS

66

Oboe — an ill woodwind that nobody blows good.
ANONYMOUS

99

Twelve highlanders and a bagpipe make a rebellion.
ANONYMOUS

66

I do not mind what language opera is sung in so long as it is in a language I don't understand.
EDWARD APPLETON

66

Brass bands are all very well in their place —
outdoors and several miles away.
THOMAS BEECHAM

99

The bagpipes sound exactly the same when you
have finished learning them as when you start.
THOMAS BEECHAM

66

The sound of the harpsichord resembles that of a
bird cage played with toasting forks.
THOMAS BEECHAM

99

There are two golden rules for an orchestra: start
together and finish together. The public doesn't give
a damn what goes on in between.
THOMAS BEECHAM

66

Piano: a parlor utensil for subduing the impenitent
visitor. It is operated by depressing the keys of the
machine and the spirits of the audience.
AMBROSE BIERCE

99

The opera isn't over till the fat lady sings.
DAN COOK

66

*People are wrong when they say the opera isn't
what it used to be. It is what it used to be.
That's what's wrong with it.*
NOEL COWARD

99

*Composers shouldn't think too much —
it interferes with their plagiarism.*
HOWARD DIETZ

66

*She was an aging singer who had to take
every note above "A" with her eyebrows.*
MONTAGUE GLASS

99

The only sensual pleasure without vice.
SAMUEL JOHNSON (on music)

66

*The conductor has the advantage of
not seeing the audience.*
ANDRÉ KOSTALENETZ

99

*What a terrible revenge by the culture
of Negroes on that of the Whites.*
IGNACY PADEREWSKI (on jazz)

66

Nothing soothes me more after a long and maddening course of pianoforte recitals than to sit and have my teeth drilled.
GEORGE BERNARD SHAW

99

Jazz will endure just as long as people hear it through their feet instead of their brains.
JOHN PHILIP SOUSA

66

Unperformed music is like a cake in the oven — not fully baked.
ISAAC STERN

99

The cello is not one of my favorite instruments. It has such a lugubrious sound, like someone reading a will.
IRENE THOMAS

66

An unalterable and unquestionable law of the musical world required that the German text of French operas sung by Swedish artists should be translated into Italian for the clearer understanding of English-speaking audiences.
EDITH WHARTON

Nature and environment

❝

*Ecology is rather like sex:
each new generation likes
to think they were the first
to discover it.*
MICHAEL ALLABY

❞

*A nature lover is a person
who, when treed by a
bear, enjoys the view.*
ANONYMOUS

❝

*A tree never hits an automobile except in
self-defense.*
ANONYMOUS

❞

*Nature never makes any blunders; when she makes
a fool she means it.*
JOSH BILLINGS

❝

Winter is nature's way of saying, "Up yours."
ROBERT BYRNE

99

Weather forecast for tonight: dark.
GEORGE CARLIN

66

I hate the outdoors. To me the outdoors is where the car is.
WILL DURST

99

Rivers in the United States are so polluted that acid rain makes them cleaner.
ANDREW MALCOLM

66

There's so much pollution in the air now that if it weren't for our lungs there'd be no place to put it all.
ROBERT ORBEN

99

A lot of people like snow. I find it to be an unnecessary freezing of water.
CARL REINER

66

The reason lightning doesn't strike twice in the same place is that the same place isn't there the second time.
WILLIE TYLER

Optimism and pessimism

"

A pessimist is one who feels bad when he feels good for fear he'll feel worse when he feels better.
ANONYMOUS

"

Always borrow from a pessimist — he never expects to get it back.
ANONYMOUS

"

An optimist sees an opportunity in every calamity; a pessimist sees a calamity in every opportunity.
ANONYMOUS

"

Every cloud has a silver lining.
ANONYMOUS

"

It will all come right in the wash.
ANONYMOUS

99

No news is good news.
ANONYMOUS

66

*Optimist: a cheerful frame of mind that enables a
tea kettle to sing though in hot water up to its nose.*
ANONYMOUS

99

Tomorrow is another day.
ANONYMOUS

66

When one door shuts, another opens.
ANONYMOUS

99

*Optimism: an intellectual disorder,
yielding to no treatment but death.
It is hereditary, but fortunately not contagious.*
AMBROSE BIERCE

66

*Optimist: a proponent of the doctrine that
black is white.*
AMBROSE BIERCE

99

*The man who can smile when things go wrong has
thought of someone he can blame it on.*
ARTHUR BLOCH

66

*The optimist proclaims we live in the best of all
possible worlds; and the pessimist fears this is true.*
JAMES BRANCH CABELL

99

*A pessimist is a man who thinks all women are bad.
An optimist is a man who hopes they are.*
CHAUNCEY DEPEW

66

*Two men look out through the same bars:
one sees the mud, and one the stars.*
FREDERICK LANGBRIDGE

99

*If we see light at the end of the tunnel it is the light
of an oncoming train.*
ROBERT LOWELL

66

*An optimist is a guy that never had much
experience.*
DON MARQUIS

99

The optimist thinks that this is the best of all possible worlds, and the pessimist knows it.
J. ROBERT OPPENHEIMER

66

A pessimist is a man who looks both ways when crossing a one-way street.
LAURENCE J. PETER

99

Do you know what a pessimist is? A man who thinks everybody is as nasty as himself, and hates them for it.
GEORGE BERNARD SHAW

66

The latest definition of an optimist is one who fills up his crossword puzzle in ink.
CLEMENT KING SHORTER

99

An optimist is one who knows exactly how bad a place the world can be; a pessimist is one who finds out anew every morning.
PETER USTINOV

66

Pessimist — one who, when he has the choice of two evils, chooses both.
OSCAR WILDE

Poets and poetry

❝

I've read some of your modern free verse and wonder who set it free.
JOHN BARRYMORE

❞

Poetry is a religion without hope.
JEAN COCTEAU

❝

Immature poets imitate; mature poets steal.
T.S. ELIOT

❞

Writing free verse is like playing tennis with the net down.
ROBERT FROST

❝

To be a poet is a condition rather than a profession.
ROBERT GRAVES

❞

A person born with an instinct for poverty.
ELBERT HUBBARD (on poets)

66

*Publishing a volume of verse is like dropping
a rose petal down the Grand Canyon
and waiting for the echo.*
DON MARQUIS

99

*The writing of more than seventy-five poems in any
fiscal year should be punishable by a fine of £500.*
ED SANDERS

66

*Having verse set to music is like looking at a
painting through a stained glass window.*
PAUL VALÉRY

99

Poetry is to prose as dancing is to walking.
JOHN WAIN

66

A poet can survive anything but a misprint.
OSCAR WILDE

99

*Poets know how useful passion is for publication.
Nowadays a broken heart will run to many editions.*
OSCAR WILDE

Politics

"

I will undoubtedly have to seek what is happily known as gainful employment, which I am glad to say does not describe holding public office.
DEAN ACHESON

"

The first requirement of a statesman is that he be dull. This is not always easy to achieve.
DEAN ACHESON

"

Politics is the gentle art of getting votes from the poor and campaign funds from the rich, by promising to protect each from the other.
OSCAR AMERINGER

"

Our Congressmen are the finest body of men money can buy.
MAURY AMSTERDAM

"

Dictators ride to and fro upon tigers from which they dare not dismount.
ANONYMOUS

"

If voting changed anything, they'd make it illegal.
ANONYMOUS

"

What is the difference between capitalism and communism? Capitalism is the exploitation of man by man; communism is the reverse.
ANONYMOUS

"

You have all the characteristics of a popular politician: a horrible voice, bad breeding, and a vulgar manner.
ARISTOPHANES

"

Democracy means government by discussion, but it is only effective if you can stop people talking.
CLEMENT ATTLEE

"

Trying to make the presidency work these days is like trying to sew buttons on a custard pie.
JAMES DAVID BARBER

66

The politician is an acrobat: he keeps his balance by saying the opposite of what he does.
MAURICE BARRÈS

99

Vote for the man who promises least; he'll be the least disappointing.
BERNARD BARUCH

66

The presidency is now a cross between a popularity contest and a high school debate, with an encyclopedia of clichés the first prize.
SAUL BELLOW

99

Politics is a blood sport.
ANEURIN BEVAN

66

We know what happens to people who stay in the middle of the road. They get run over.
ANEURIN BEVAN

99

Alliance: in international politics, the union of two thieves who have their hands so deeply inserted into each other's pocket that they cannot safely plunder a third.
AMBROSE BIERCE

"

Conservative: a statesman who is enamored of existing evils, as distinguished from the liberal, who wishes to replace them with others.
AMBROSE BIERCE

"

We should really call all politicans actors.
MARLON BRANDO

"

I believe in benevolent dictatorship provided I am the dictator.
RICHARD BRANSON

"

Anybody that wants the presidency so much that he'll spend two years organizing and campaigning for it is not to be trusted with the office.
DAVID BRODER

"

If presidents don't do it to their wives, they'll do it to the country.
MEL BROOKS

"

A liberal is a man who leaves a room when the fight begins.
HEYWOOD BROUN

❝

Too bad all the people who know how to run the country are busy driving cabs and cutting hair.
GEORGE BURNS

❞

If you think you have someone eating out of your hand, it's a good idea to count your fingers.
MARTIN BUXBAUME

❝

Democracy is being allowed to vote for the candidate you dislike least.
ROBERT BYRNE

❞

An honest politician is one who, when he is bought, will stay bought.
SIMON CAMERON

❝

The only good government is a bad one in a hell of a fright.
JOYCE CARY

❞

Nobody believes a rumor here in Washington until it's officially denied.
EDWARD CHEYFITZ

"

*An appeaser is one who feeds a crocodile —
hoping that it will eat him last.*
WINSTON CHURCHILL

"

*It has been said that democracy
is the worst form of government
except all the others that have been tried.*
WINSTON CHURCHILL

"

*The ability to foretell what's going to happen
tomorrow, next week, next month, and next year.
And to have the ability afterwards to explain
why it didn't happen.*
WINSTON CHURCHILL (on political skill)

"

*One of the luxuries of a politician's life is that you
see yourself as others see you.*
JOE CLARK

"

*Political thinking consists in deciding upon
the conclusion first and then
finding good arguments for it.*
RICHARD CROSSMAN

99

*Politics. The diplomatic name for
the law of the jungle.*
ELY CULBERTSON

66

*Get all the fools on your side and you can be
elected to anything.*
FRANK DANE

99

*I have come to the conclusion that politics are too
serious a matter to be left to the politicians.*
CHARLES DE GAULLE

66

*In order to become the master,
the politician poses as the servant.*
CHARLES DE GAULLE

99

*In politics it is necessary either to betray one's
country or the electorate.*
CHARLES DE GAULLE

66

*Dirksen's Three Laws of Politics: 1. Get elected.
2. Get re-elected. 3. Don't get mad, get even.*
EVERETT DIRKSEN

99

*The trouble with socialists is that they let their
bleeding hearts go to their bloody heads.*
TOMMY DOUGLAS

66

*Now I know what a statesman is: he's a dead
politician. We need more statesmen.*
BOB EDWARDS

99

*The middle of the road is all of the usable surface.
The extremes, right and left, are in the gutters.*
DWIGHT D. EISENHOWER

66

*What counts is not necessarily the size of the dog in
the fight — it's the size of the fight in the dog.*
DWIGHT D. EISENHOWER

99

*Democracy is the name we give the people
whenever we need them.*
ROBERT, MARQUIS DE FLERS AND
ARMAND DE CAILLAVET

66

*In rivers and bad governments the lightest things
swim at the top.*
BENJAMIN FRANKLIN

99

*A liberal is a man too broadminded
to take his own side in a quarrel.*
ROBERT FROST

66

*In politics, as on the sickbed, people toss from side
to side, thinking they will be more comfortable.*
JOHANN W. VON GOETHE

99

To rule is easy, to govern difficult.
JOHANN W. VON GOETHE

66

*Diplomacy is to do and say
The nastiest thing in the nicest way.*
ISAAC GOLDBERG

99

*A government that is big enough to give you all you
want is big enough to take it all away.*
BARRY GOLDWATER

66

*Probably the most distinctive characteristic of the
successful politician is selective cowardice.*
RICHARD HARRIS

99

What is politics but persuading the public to vote for this and support that and endure these for the promise of those?
GILBERT HIGHET

66

What luck for rulers that men do not think.
ADOLF HITLER

99

Government: a kind of legalized pillage.
KIN HUBBARD

66

It is useless for the sheep to pass resolutions in favour of vegetarianism while the wolf remains of a different opinion.
WILLIAM R. INGE

99

When we got into office, the thing that surprised me most was to find that things were just as bad as we'd been saying they were.
JOHN F. KENNEDY

66

Politicians are the same everywhere. They promise to build bridges even where there are no rivers.
NIKITA KHRUSHCHEV

99

Ninety percent of the politicians give the other ten percent a bad reputation.
HENRY KISSINGER

66

The illegal we do immediately.
The unconstitutional takes a little longer.
HENRY KISSINGER

99

There cannot be a crisis next week.
My schedule is already full.
HENRY KISSINGER

66

What this country needs is more unemployed politicians.
EDWARD LANGLEY

99

To lead people, walk behind them.
LAO-TZU

66

I've got to follow them — I am their leader.
ALEXANDRE LEDRU-ROLLIN

99

I once said cynically of a politician, "He'll doublecross that bridge when he comes to it."
OSCAR LEVANT

66

A dilemma is a politician trying to save both sides of his face at once.
JOHN A. LINCOLN

99

A politician is a person with whose politics you don't agree; if you agree with him, he is a statesman.
DAVID LLOYD GEORGE

66

This organization (the United Nations) *is created to prevent you from going to hell. It isn't created to take you to heaven.*
HENRY CABOT LODGE, JR.

99

It was a storm in a tea cup, but in politics we sail in paper boats.
HAROLD MACMILLAN

"

*Congress is so strange. A man gets up to
speak and says nothing. Nobody listens —
and then everybody disagrees.*
BORIS MARSHALOV

"

*It is very unfair to expect a politician
to live in private
up to the statements he makes in public.*
W. SOMERSET MAUGHAM

"

*Politician: any citizen with influence
enough to get his old mother a job
as charwoman in the City Hall.*
H.L. MENCKEN

"

*There are some politicians who,
if their constituents were cannibals,
would promise them missionaries for dinner.*
H.L. MENCKEN

"

*Voting is simply a way of determining
which side is the stronger
without putting it to the test of fighting.*
H.L. MENCKEN

99

One day the don't-knows will get in, and then where will we be?
SPIKE MILLIGAN

66

Any party which takes credit for the rain must not be surprised if its opponents blame it for the drought.
DWIGHT W. MORROW

99

There are two levers for moving men — interest and fear.
NAPOLEON BONAPARTE

66

Democracy is good. I say this because other systems are worse.
JAWAHARLAL NEHRU

99

A politician divides mankind into two classes: tools and enemies.
FRIEDRICH W. NIETZSCHE

66

I would have made a good Pope.
RICHARD NIXON

99

*A conservative is a man who
wants the rules changed so
that no one can make a pile the way he did.*
GREGORY NUNN

66

*A statesman shears the sheep,
the politician skins them.*
AUSTIN O'MALLEY

99

*Politicians are like the bones of a horse's
foreshoulder — not a straight one in it.*
WENDELL PHILLIPS

66

*Those who are too smart to engage in politics
are punished by being governed by those
who are dumber.*
PLATO

99

*A communist is a person who
publicly airs his dirty Lenin.*
JACK POMEROY

66

*A statesman is a politician who places himself at
the service of the nation. A politician is a
statesman who places the nation at his service.*
GEORGES POMPIDOU

99

*Government is like a baby. An alimentary canal
with a big appetite at one end and no sense of
responsibility at the other.*
RONALD REAGAN

66

*I have left orders to be awakened at any time
in case of national emergency,
even if I'm in a cabinet meeting.*
RONALD REAGAN

99

*I used to say that politics was the second oldest
profession, and I have come to know that it bears a
gross similarity to the first.*
RONALD REAGAN

66

*The taxpayer, that's someone who works for
the federal government, but doesn't have to take a
civil service examination.*
RONALD REAGAN

99

*The government is the only known vessel
that leaks from the top.*
JAMES RESTON

66

Politics has got so expensive that it takes a lot of money even to get beat with.
WILL ROGERS

99

This country has come to feel the same when Congress is in session as when the baby gets hold of a hammer.
WILL ROGERS

66

There is a homely adage which runs, "Speak softly and carry a big stick, you will go far."
THEODORE ROOSEVELT

99

To prevent resentment, governments attribute misfortunes to natural causes; to create resentment, oppositions attribute them to human causes.
BERTRAND RUSSELL

66

Liberals feel unworthy of their possessions. Conservatives feel they deserve everything they've stolen.
MORT SAHL

99

A politician . . . one that would circumvent God.
WILLIAM SHAKESPEARE

66

Democracy subsitutes selection by the incompetent many for appointment by the corrupt few.
GEORGE BERNARD SHAW

99

He knows nothing; he thinks he knows everything – that clearly points to a political career.
GEORGE BERNARD SHAW

66

An independent is a guy who wants to take the politics out of politics.
ADLAI STEVENSON

99

In America, anyone can become president. That's one of the risks you take.
ADLAI STEVENSON

66

Your public servants serve you right.
ADLAI STEVENSON

99

Politics is perhaps the only profession for which no preparation is thought necessary.
ROBERT LOUIS STEVENSON

❝

If you want to understand democracy, spend less time in the library with Plato, and more time in the buses with people.
SIMEON STRUNSKY

❞

In politics, if you want anything said, ask a man; if you want anything done, ask a woman.
MARGARET THATCHER

❝

You can fool too many of the people too much of the time.
JAMES THURBER

❞

Suppose you were an idiot and suppose you were a member of Congress. But I repeat myself.
MARK TWAIN

❝

Money is the mother's milk of politics.
JESSE UNRUH

❞

A diplomat these days is nothing but a headwaiter who's allowed to sit down occasionally.
PETER USTINOV

"

*A statesman is any politician it's considered safe to
name a school after.*
BILL VAUGHAN

"

*It is dangerous to be right
when the government is wrong.*
VOLTAIRE

"

*The best government is a benevolent tyranny
tempered by an occasional assassination.*
VOLTAIRE

"

*The Labour Party is going about the
country stirring up apathy.*
WILLIAM WHITELAW

"

*Democracy means simply the bludgeoning of the
people by the people for the people.*
OSCAR WILDE

"

*An ambassador is an honest man sent to lie abroad
for the good of his country.*
HENRY WOTTON

Prejudice

"

*If we were to wake up
some morning and find
that everyone
was the same race,
creed and color,
we would find some other
causes for prejudice
by noon.*
GEORGE AIKEN

"

*Our prejudices are our
mistresses; reason is at
best our wife,
very often heard indeed,
but seldom minded.*
LORD CHESTERFIELD

"

*He had only one eye, and the popular prejudice
runs in favor of two.*
CHARLES DICKENS

"

*Common sense is the collection of prejudices
acquired by age eighteen.*
ALBERT EINSTEIN

66

I am free of all prejudices. I hate everyone equally.
W.C. FIELDS

99

A fox should not be on the jury at a goose's trial.
THOMAS FULLER

66

*I never believed in Santa Claus
because I knew no white dude
would come into my neighborhood after dark.*
DICK GREGORY

99

*The mind of the bigot is like the pupil of the eye;
the more light you pour upon it,
the more it will contract.*
OLIVER WENDELL HOLMES

66

*Nothing is so firmly believed as
that which is least known.*
MICHEL DE MONTAIGNE

99

All looks yellow to a jaundiced eye.
ALEXANDER POPE

Quoting

66

*Hush, little bright line,
don't you cry, You'll be a
cliché by and by.*
FRED ALLEN

99

*Quoting: the act of
repeating erroneously the
words of another.*
AMBROSE BIERCE

66

*Shake was a dramatist of note;
He lived by writing things to quote.*
H.C. BUNNER

99

*You could compile the worst book in the world
entirely out of selected passages from the best
writers in the world.*
G.K. CHESTERTON

66

The wise make proverbs and fools repeat them.
ISAAC D'ISRAELI

99

Stronger than an army is a quotation whose time has come.
W.I.E. GATES

66

The difference between my quotations and those of the next man is that I leave out the inverted commas.
GEORGE MOORE

99

He liked those literary cooks
Who skim the cream of other's books;
And ruin half an author's graces
By plucking bon-mots from their places.
HANNAH MORE

66

Misquotations are the only quotations that are never misquoted.
HESKETH PEARSON

99

I often quote myself. It adds spice to my conversation.
GEORGE BERNARD SHAW

66

Some, for renown, on scraps of learning dote, And think they grow immortal as they quote.
EDWARD YOUNG

Religion

> **❝**
> *Most of us spend the first six days of each week sowing wild oats, then we go to church on Sunday and pray for a crop failure.*
> FRED ALLEN
> **❞**

> *God helps those who help themselves.*
> ANONYMOUS

> **❝**
> *God is alive. He just doesn't want to get involved.*
> ANONYMOUS
> **❞**

> *I know I am God, because when I pray to Him I am talking to myself.*
> ANONYMOUS

> **❝**
> *If God lived on earth, people would break his windows.*
> ANONYMOUS

99

*May you get to heaven a half hour before
the Devil knows you're dead.*
ANONYMOUS

66

We didn't invent sin. We're just trying to perfect it.
ANONYMOUS

99

*Every man thinks God is on his side.
The rich and the powerful know that he is.*
JEAN ANOUILH

66

*O Lord, thou knowest how busy I must be this day;
if I forget thee, do not thou forget me.*
SIR JACOB ASTLEY

99

If it's heaven for climate, it's hell for company.
J.M. BARRIE

66

*God is not dead but alive and working on
a much less ambitious project.*
PETER BARNES

99

*The wicked often work harder to go to hell
than the righteous do to enter heaven.*
JOSH BILLINGS

66

*When something good happens it's a
miracle and you should wonder what God is
saving up for you later.*
MARSHALL BRICKMAN

99

*Every day people are straying away from the
Church and going back to God.*
LENNY BRUCE

66

*An atheist is a man who has no invisible
means of support.*
JOHN BUCHAN

99

Thanks to God, I am still an atheist.
LUIS BUNUEL

66

*A church is a hospital for sinners,
not a museum for saints.*
ABIGAIL VAN BUREN

99

*An apology for the Devil: it must be remembered
that we have only heard one side of the case.
God has written all the books.*
SAMUEL BUTLER

66

*Everyone is as God made him, and
often a great deal worse.*
MIGUEL DE CERVANTES

99

*The Bible tells us to love our neighbors, and also
to love our enemies; probably because they are
generally the same people.*
G.K. CHESTERTON

66

*The Christian ideal has not been tried and found
wanting; it has been found difficult and left untried.*
G.K. CHESTERTON

99

*Wherever God erects a house of prayer,
The Devil always builds a chapel there;
And 'twill be found, upon examination,
The latter has the largest congregation.*
DANIEL DEFOE

66

*It is no accident that the symbol of a
bishop is a crook and the sign of an
archbishop is a double-cross.*
DOM GREGORY DIX

99

*Most people have some sort of religion — at least
they know what Church they're staying away from.*
JOHN ERSKINE

66

*Christ died for our sins. Dare we make his
martyrdom meaningless by not committing them?*
JULES FEIFFER

99

I'm an agnostic — means I don't know the answers.
HENRY FONDA

66

*As I take my shoes from the shoemaker,
and my coat from the tailor, so I take my
religion from the priest.*
OLIVER GOLDSMITH

99

*It was a divine sermon. For it was like the peace of
God — which passeth all understanding. And like
his mercy, it seemed to endure forever.*
HENRY HAWKINS

"

*It needs more than a mere opinion to
erect a Gothic cathedral.*
HEINRICH HEINE

"

*Priests are no more necessary to religion
than politicians to patriotism.*
JOHN HAYNES HOLMES

"

*A miracle: an event described by those to whom
it was told by men who did not see it.*
ELBERT HUBBARD

"

*The inspiration of the Bible depends on the
ignorance of the person who reads it.*
ROBERT G. INGERSOLL

"

With soap baptism is a good thing.
ROBERT G. INGERSOLL

"

*My dear child, you must believe in God
inspite of what the clergy tell you.*
BENJAMIN JOWETT

66

*God seems to have left the receiver off
the hook and time is running out.*
ARTHUR KOESTLER

99

*I believe in God, in the family, and in McDonald's.
And at the office that order is reversed.*
RAY KROC

66

*What a pity that the only way to
heaven is in a hearse!*
STANISLAW J. LEC

99

God is love, but get it in writing.
GYPSY ROSE LEE

66

*A converted cannibal is one who, on Friday,
eats only fishermen.*
EMILY LOTNEY

99

*A Sunday school is a prison in which children do
penance for the evil conscience of their parents.*
H.L. MENCKEN

66

Archbishop: a Christian ecclesiastic of a rank superior to that attained by Christ.
H.L. MENCKEN

99

We must respect the other fellow's religion, but only in the sense and to the extent that we respect his theory that his wife is beautiful and his children smart.
H.L. MENCKEN

66

God help those who do not help themselves.
ADDISON MIZNER

99

I respect faith, but doubt is what gets you an education.
WILSON MIZNER

66

If triangles made a god, they would give him three sides.
BARON MONTESQUIEU

99

My theology, briefly, is that the universe was dictated but not signed.
CHRISTOPHER MORLEY

66

Religion is a candle inside a multicolored lantern. Everyone looks through a particular color, but the candle is still there.
MUHAMMAD NAGUIB

99

Living with a saint is more grueling than being one.
ROBERT NEVILLE

66

Christ: an anarchist who succeeded. That's all.
FRIEDRICH W. NIETZSCHE

99

In heaven all the interesting people are missing.
FRIEDRICH W. NIETZSCHE

66

The last Christian died on the cross.
FRIEDRICH W. NIETZSCHE

99

Which is it: is man one of God's blunders, or is God one of man's blunders?
FRIEDRICH W. NIETZSCHE

"

Going to church doesn't make you a Christian any more than going to the garage makes you a car.
LAURENCE J. PETER

"

God is really only another artist. He invented the giraffe, the elephant, the cat. He has no real style. He just goes on trying other things.
PABLO PICASSO

"

Man is great only when he is kneeling.
POPE PIUS XII

"

I think sermons would be better if the clergy did not preach quite so much.
DR. MICHAEL RAMSAY

"

Jesus was a Jew, yes, but only on his mother's side.
STANLEY RALPH ROSS

"

The worst moment for the atheist is when he is really thankful and has nobody to thank.
DANTE GABRIEL ROSSETTI

66

*People may say what they like about the decay of
Christianity; the religious system that produced
green Chartreuse can never really die.*
SAKI

99

*Why attack God? He may be as
miserable as we are.*
ERIK SATIE

66

*A man does not have to be an angel
in order to be a saint.*
ALBERT SCHWEITZER

99

*The fact that a believer is happier than a skeptic
is no more to the point than the fact that a
drunken man is happier than a sober one.*
GEORGE BERNARD SHAW

66

*As the French say, there are three sexes —
men, women, and clergymen.*
SYDNEY SMITH

99

The world is proof that God is a committee.
BOB STOKES

66

If you talk to God, you are praying; if God talks to you, you have schizophrenia.
THOMAS SZASZ

99

When I think of the number of disagreeable people that I know who have gone to a better world, I am sure hell won't be so bad at all.
MARK TWAIN

66

God made everything out of nothing, but the nothingness shows through.
PAUL VALÉRY

99

If God created us in his own image, we have more than reciprocated.
VOLTAIRE

66

A Christian is a man who feels repentance on a Sunday for what he did on Saturday and is going to do on Monday.
THOMAS R. YBARRA

99

Every dogma has its day.
ISRAEL ZANGWILL

Religion: proverbs

A piece of the churchyard fits everybody.

All are not saints who go to church.

Better to go to heaven in rags than to hell in embroidery.

Dung is no saint, but where it falls it works miracles.

Hell is always open.

In church, or an inn, or a coffin, all men are equal.

It is good to lend to God and the soil — they pay good interest.

Late repentance is seldom worth much.

Offend one monk, and the hoods of all monks' cloaks will flutter as far as Rome.

Poor men will go to heaven as soon as the rich.

Priests and women never forget.

St. Luke was a saint and a physician, and yet he died.

The best way to travel is toward heaven.

The devil tempts all, but the idle man tempts the devil.

Throw not thy hatchet at the Lord — He will turn the sharp edge against thee.

To God's council-chamber there is no key.

What the church does not take the taxman does.

When God means to punish a nation, He deprives its rulers of wisdom.

Where God builds a church the devil builds a chapel.

Wherever there is mischief, there is sure to be a priest and a woman in it.

Science and technology

"

*If the human race wants
to go to Hell in a basket,
technology can help it
get there by jet.*
CHARLES M. ALLEN

"

*A drug is a substance that
when injected into a
guinea pig produces a
scientific paper.*
ANONYMOUS

"

A stitch in time would have confused Einstein.
ANONYMOUS

"

*For people who like peace and quiet:
a phoneless cord.*
ANONYMOUS

"

*Horsepower was a wonderful thing
when only horses had it.*
ANONYMOUS

99

Life is extinct on other planets because their scientists were more advanced than ours.
ANONYMOUS

66

There is no gravity. The earth sucks.
ANONYMOUS

99

Time is nature's way of keeping everything from happening at once.
ANONYMOUS

66

That's one small step for man, one giant leap for mankind.
NEIL ARMSTRONG

99

When I find myself in the company of scientists, I feel like a shabby curate who has strayed by mistake into a drawing room full of dukes.
W.H. AUDEN

66

Inanimate objects are classified scientifically into three major categories — those that don't work, those that break down, and those that get lost.
RUSSELL BAKER

99

*Research is the process of going up alleys
to see if they are blind.*
MARSTON BATES

66

*The people who live in the past
must yield to the people who live in the future.
Otherwise the world would begin
to turn the other way round.*
ARNOLD BENNETT

99

*The factory of the future will have only two
employees, a man and a dog.
The man will be there to feed the dog.
The dog will be there to keep the man from
touching the equipment.*
WARREN G. BENNIS

66

*A blind man in a dark room —
looking for a black hat — which isn't there.*
CHARLES SYNGE CHRISTOPHER BOWEN (on a
metaphysician)

99

*Eve and the apple was the first great step in
experimental science.*
JAMES BRIDIE

66

There was a young lady named Bright,
Whose speed was far faster than light;
She set out one day
In a relative way,
And returned home the previous night.
ARTHUR HENRY REGINALD BULLER

99

Everything is in a state of flux,
including the status quo.
ROBERT BYRNE

66

I shall make electricity so cheap that only
the rich can afford to burn candles.
THOMAS EDISON

99

Technological progress is like an axe in the hands
of a pathological criminal.
ALBERT EINSTEIN

66

When you are courting a nice girl an hour seems
like a second. When you sit on a red-hot cinder a
second seems like an hour. That's relativity.
ALBERT EINSTEIN

99

Law of the Hydrodynamics: When the body is immersed in water, the telephone rings.
CAMILLE FLAMMARION

66

The most popular labor-saving device is still money.
PHYLLIS GEORGE

99

The World would be a safer place,
If someone had a plan,
Before exploring Outer Space,
To find the Inner Man.
E.Y. HARBURG

66

As the horsepower in modern automobiles steadily rises, the congestion of traffic steadily lowers the possible speed of your car. This is known as Progress.
SYDNEY J. HARRIS

99

The thing with high-tech is that you always end up using scissors.
DAVID HOCKNEY

66

Some things have to be believed to be seen.
RALPH HODGSON (on ESP)

99

*It is said that one machine can do the work of
fifty ordinary men. No machine, however, can do
the work of one extraordinary man.*
TEHYI HSIEH

66

*Science has "explained" nothing;
the more we know the more fantastic
the world becomes and the profounder the
surrounding darkness.*
ALDOUS HUXLEY

99

*The great tragedy of Science — the slaying of a
beautiful hypothesis by an ugly fact.*
T.H. HUXLEY

66

*Put three grains of sand inside a vast cathedral,
and the cathedral will be more closely packed with
sand than space is with stars.*
JAMES JEANS

99

*I am sorry to say there is too much point
to the wise crack that life is extinct
on other planets because their
scientists were more advanced than ours.*
JOHN F. KENNEDY

66

*This is the machine age. The only thing people do
by hand is scratch themselves.*
JOE LAURIE, JR.

99

*Scientists are rarely to be counted
among the fun people. Awkward at parties,
shy with strangers, deficient in irony —
they have had no choice but to turn their attention
to the study of everyday objects.*
FRAN LEBOWITZ

66

*Xerox: A trademark for a photocopying device
that can make rapid reproductions
of human error, perfectly.*
MERLE L. MEACHAM

99

*If I have seen further it is by standing on the
shoulders of giants.*
ISAAC NEWTON

66

*One has to look out for engineers —
they begin with sewing machines
and end up with the atomic bomb.*
MARCEL PAGNOL

99

*Science is built up of facts, as a house is built of
stones; but an accumulation of facts is no more a
science than a heap of stones is a house.*
HENRI POINCARÉ

66

*There are three roads to ruin —
women, gambling, and technicians.
The most pleasant is with women,
the quickest is with gambling,
but the surest is with technicians.*
GEORGES POMPIDOU

99

*The scientific theory I like best
is that the rings of Saturn are composed
entirely of lost airline luggage.*
MIKE RUSSELL

66

*Electric clocks reveal to you
Precisely when your fuses blew.*
LEONARD SCHIFF

99

*Discovery consists of seeing what everybody has
seen and thinking what nobody has thought.*
ALBERT VON SZENT-GYÖRGYI

Sex

66

*Too many cooks spoil
the brothel.*
POLLY ADLER

99

*I have to find a girl
attractive or it's like
trying to start a car
without an ignition key.*
JONATHAN AITKEN

66

*Bisexuality immediately doubles your chances
for a date on Saturday night.*
WOODY ALLEN

99

*Don't knock masturbation —
it's sex with someone I love.*
WOODY ALLEN

66

*I want to tell you a terrific story about
oral contraception. I asked this girl to sleep
with me and she said "no."*
WOODY ALLEN

99

Is sex dirty? Only if it's done right.
WOODY ALLEN

66

*Love is the answer, but while you are waiting for
the answer, sex raises some pretty good questions.*
WOODY ALLEN

99

*Sex is like having dinner: sometimes you joke about
the dishes, sometimes you take the meal seriously.*
WOODY ALLEN

66

Flies spread disease — so keep yours zipped.
ANONYMOUS

99

*Sex with a man is all right, but it's not as
good as the real thing.*
ANONYMOUS

66

*Women don't smoke after sex because one
drag a night is enough.*
ANONYMOUS

99

*The prostitute is the only honest
woman left in America.*
TI-GRACE ATKINSON

66

*It's the good girls who keep the diaries;
the bad girls never have the time.*
TALLULAH BANKHEAD

99

*Sex: the thing that takes up the least amount of
time and causes the most amount of trouble.*
JOHN BARRYMORE

66

*Sex is like money — very nice to have
but vulgar to talk about.*
TONIA BERG

99

*If God had meant us to have group sex,
he'd have given us more organs.*
MALCOLM BRADBURY

66

*It's not all that important to me. It would be
important if I wasn't getting any.*
MICHAEL CAINE

99

*The pleasure is momentary, the position
ridiculous, and the expense damnable.*
LORD CHESTERFIELD

66

*Sex is like pizza. Even when it's bad
it's still pretty good.*
HELEN CHILDRESS

99

God's biggest joke on human beings.
BETTE DAVIS

66

*In America sex is an obsession, in other parts
of the world it is a fact.*
MARLENE DIETRICH

99

*The big difference between sex for money
and sex for free is that sex for money
usually costs a lot less.*
BRENDAN FRANCIS

66

People who throw kisses are hopelessly lazy.
BOB HOPE

99

*Chastity: the most unnatural of the
sexual perversions.*
ALDOUS HUXLEY

66

*The trouble with Ian is that he gets off with
women because he can't get on with them.*
ROSAMUND LEHMANN (on Ian Fleming)

99

*A promiscuous person is someone who is
getting more sex than you are.*
VICTOR LOWNES

66

*Whoever named it necking was a poor
judge of anatomy.*
GROUCHO MARX

99

*It has to be admitted that we English have
sex on the brain, which is a very
unsatisfactory place to have it.*
MALCOLM MUGGERIDGE

66

*You know, she speaks eighteen languages.
And she can't say "no" in any of them.*
DOROTHY PARKER

99

Sex is the biggest nothing of all time.
ANDY WARHOL

66

All this fuss about sleeping together.
For physical pleasure
I'd sooner go to my dentist any day.
EVELYN WAUGH

99

An orgasm a day keeps the doctor away.
MAE WEST

66

Give a man a free hand and he'll
run it all over you.
MAE WEST

99

When women go wrong, men go right after them.
MAE WEST

66

I thought coq au vin *was love in a lorry.*
VICTORIA WOOD

Sport and games

> **"**
>
> *If horses can't eat it,*
> *I won't play on it.*
> DICK ALLEN (on Astroturf)
>
> **"**

> *A cricket bat is an*
> *instrument that looks like*
> *a baseball bat run over*
> *by a steamroller.*
> ANONYMOUS

> **"**
>
> *A football coach is a person who is willing to lay*
> *down your life for the good of his team.*
> ANONYMOUS

> **"**
>
> *American professional athletes are bilingual:*
> *they speak English and profanity.*
> ANONYMOUS

> **"**
>
> *Croquet is like embalming fluid. It keeps you*
> *in the same state forever.*
> ANONYMOUS

99

Fishing is the sport of drowning worms.
ANONYMOUS

66

Old skaters never die, they just lose their ice sight.
ANONYMOUS

99

Rugby is played by men with odd shaped balls.
ANONYMOUS

66

Running is an unnatural act, except from enemies and to the bathroom.
Anonymous

99

The difference between learning to play golf and learning to drive an automobile is that in golf you never hit anything.
ANONYMOUS

66

The hardest thing about roller skating is the ground.
ANONYMOUS

99

Skiing is the only sport where you can spend an arm and a leg to break an arm and a leg.
HENRY BEARD

66

The formal term for a collection of fishermen is an exaggeration of anglers.
HENRY BEARD

99

Give me my golf clubs, fresh air, and a beautiful partner, and you can keep my golf clubs and the fresh air.
JACK BENNY

66

You can't think and hit the ball at the same time.
LAWRENCE PETER "YOGI" BERRA

99

When I was forty my doctor advised me that a man in his forties shouldn't play tennis. I heeded his advice carefully and could hardly wait until I reached fifty to start again.
HUGO L. BLACK

66

I do not participate in any sport with ambulances at the bottom of the hill.
ERMA BOMBECK (on skiing)

99

*This is a sport where you talk about sequins,
earrings, and plunging necklines —
and you are talking about the men.*
CHRISTINE BRENNAN (on ice skating)

66

*I am still looking for shoes that will make
running on streets seem like running
barefoot across the bosoms of maidens.*
DAVE BROSNAN

99

*A puck is a hard rubber disk that hockey players
strike when they can't hit each other.*
JIMMY CANNON

66

*The trouble with officials is they just
don't care who wins.*
TOMMY CANTERBURY

99

*I regard golf as an expensive way
of playing marbles.*
G.K. CHESTERTON

66

*Golf is an ineffectual attempt to direct an
uncontrollable sphere into an inaccessible hole
with instruments ill-adapted to the purpose.*
WINSTON CHURCHILL

99

*If God had meant football to be played in the air,
he'd have put grass in the sky.*
BRIAN CLOUGH (on soccer)

66

*I was once knocked out by a Mexican
bantamweight — six of my pals were
swinging him around by his heels at the time.*
RANDALL "TEX" COB

99

*I went to a fight the other evening
and an ice hockey game broke out.*
RODNEY DANGERFIELD

66

*Football is not a contact sport.
It's a collision sport.*
DUFFY DAUGHERTY

99

Old card-players never die, they simply shuffle off.
FELICIA DeMARTIN

66

My idea of exercise is a good brisk sit.
PHYLLIS DILLER

99

*The reason the pro tells you to keep your head
down is so you can't see him laughing.*
PHYLLIS DILLER (on golf)

66

*Some teams are so negative they
could be sponsored by Kodak.*
TOMMY DOCHERTY

99

*To describe the agony of a marathon to somebody
who's never run it is like trying to explain color to
a person who was born blind.*
JEROME DRAYTON

66

*Dressing a pool player in a tuxedo is like
putting whipped cream on a hot dog.*
MINNESOTA FATS

99

*Being the manager of a touring team is rather like
being in charge of a cemetery — lots of people
underneath you, but no one listening.*
WES HALL (on cricket)

66

*Cricket is a tough and terrible, rough,
unscrupulous game. No wonder our
American friends do not like it.*
A.P. HERBERT

99

*College football is a sport that bears the
same relation to education that bullfighting
does to agriculture.*
ELBERT HUBBARD

66

*I'll bet th' hardest thing 'bout prize fightin' is
pickin' up yer teeth with a boxin' glove on.*
KIN HUBBARD

99

*Putting an ex-fighter in the business world is
like putting silk stockings on a pig.*
JACK HURLEY

66

*An angler is a man who spends his rainy
days sitting around on the muddy banks of
rivers doing nothing because his wife won't let
him do it at home.*
THE IRISH NEWS

"

Old chess players never die,
they simply go to pieces.
COLIN M. JARMAN

"

Old golfers never die, they simply putter away.
COLIN M. JARMAN

"

Old ski-jumpers never die, they simply
lose their inclination.
COLIN M. JARMAN

"

Watching baseball is like . . . watching grass —
no, Astroturf — grow.
JEFF JARVIS

"

Bobsledding is a sport in which demented
people sit on a sled that goes 2,000 miles per
hour down an ice ditch. The same sport is
often practiced without ice — when four drunks
leave a fraternity party in a BMW.
DAN JENKINS

"

This bowler's like my dog: three short legs and
balls that swing each way.
BRIAN JOHNSTON (on cricket)

❝

Its a funny kind of month, October. For the keen cricket fan it's when you realize your wife left you in May.
DENIS NORDEN

❞

Fishermen and hypochondriacs have one thing in common — they don't have to catch anything to be happy.
ROBERT ORBEN

❝

A trout is a fish mainly known by hearsay. It lives on anything not included in a fisherman's equipment.
H.I. PHILIPS

❞

Exactly how intricate a sport is jogging? You were two years old; you ran after the cat; you pretty much had it mastered.
RICK REILLY

❝

If God had meant me to exercise, He'd put diamonds on the floor.
JOAN RIVERS

99

Football kickers are like taxi cabs. You can always go out and hire another one.
BUDDY RYAN

66

When a man wants to murder a tiger he calls it sport; when the tiger wants to murder him he calls it ferocity.
GEORGE BERNARD SHAW

99

Playing polo is like trying to play golf during an earthquake.
SYLVESTER STALLONE

66

It has always been my private conviction that any man who pits his intelligence against a fish and loses has it coming.
JOHN STEINBECK

99

Being a decathlete is like having ten girlfriends. You have to love them all, and you can't afford losing one.
DALEY THOMPSON

66

*Most people think that volleyball is twenty-two
people on the beach who quit playing when
the hamburgers are ready.*
STEVE TIMMONS

99

*Behind every good decathlete,
there's a good doctor.*
BILL TOOMEY

66

Golf is a good walk spoiled.
MARK TWAIN

99

*As a nation we are dedicated to keeping
physically fit — and parking as close
to the stadium as possible.*
BILL VAUGHAN

66

*This is the second most exciting indoor sport, and
the other shouldn't have spectators.*
DICK VERTLIEB (on basketball)

99

*Baseball is the favorite American sport because
it's so slow. Any idiot can follow it. And just
about any idiot can play it.*
GORE VIDAL

66

Soccer is to sport what athlete's foot is to injuries.
TOM WEIR

99

If it's all-in, why do they wrestle?
MAE WEST

66

*Football is all very well as a game for rough girls,
but it is hardly suitable for delicate boys.*
OSCAR WILDE (on soccer)

99

*Football combines the two worst features of
American life. It is violence punctuated by
committee meetings.*
GEORGE F. WILL

66

*They thought lacrosse was what
you did in la church.*
ROBIN WILLIAMS

99

*Jogging is for people who aren't intelligent
enough to watch breakfast television.*
VICTORIA WOOD

Statistics

"

*A statistician is someone
who can put his head in
the oven and his feet in
the freezer and tell you,
"On average,
I feel just fine."*
ANONYMOUS

"

*Statistics: a group of
numbers looking for an
argument.*
ANONYMOUS

"

*If you add all the breasts in the world
and all the balls,
then divide by the world population,
you prove that on average
every human has one breast and one ball.*
ANONYMOUS

"

*There are three kinds of lies: lies,
damned lies, and statistics.*
BENJAMIN DISRAELI

"

Figures won't lie, but liars will figure.
CHARLES H. GROSVENOR

"

*He uses statistics as a drunken man uses lampposts
— for support rather than for illumination.*
ANDREW LANG

"

*Statistics are like a bikini.
What they reveal is suggestive,
but what they conceal is vital.*
AARON LEVENSTEIN

"

Statistics will prove anything, even the truth.
NOEL MOYNIHAN

"

Facts are stubborn, but statistics are more pliable.
LAURENCE J. PETER

"

*A single death is a tragedy,
a million deaths is a statistic.*
JOSEPH STALIN

Success and failure

"

Success is like dealing with your kid or teaching your wife to drive. Sooner or later you'll end up in the police station.
FRED ALLEN

"

If fortune turns against you, even jelly breaks your tooth.
ANONYMOUS

"

It takes time to be a success, but time is all it takes.
ANONYMOUS

"

Show me a good loser and I'll show you a loser.
ANONYMOUS

"

The penalty of success is to be bored by people who used to snub you.
NANCY ASTOR

99

Many a man owes his success to his first wife and his second wife to his success.
JIM BACKUS

66

The secret of success is sincerity. Once you can fake that you've got it made.
A. BLOCH

99

If you want a place in the sun, prepare to put up with a few blisters.
ABIGAIL VAN BUREN

66

It takes twenty years to become an overnight success.
EDDIE CANTOR

99

Success took me to her bosom like a maternal boa constrictor.
NOEL COWARD

66

The best way to get on in the world is to make people believe it's to their advantage to help you.
JEAN DE LA BRUYÈRE

99

*It's them as take advantage that get
advantage in this world.*
GEORGE ELIOT

66

*What is success? It is a toy balloon among
children armed with pins.*
GENE FOWLER

99

*The first law of holes: When you're in a hole,
you have to stop digging.*
BENJAMIN FRANKLIN

66

*Those who tell you it's tough at the top have
never been at the bottom.*
JOE HARVEY

99

*Success is not the result of spontaneous
combustion. You must set yourself on fire.*
REGGIE LEACH

66

*There is an old motto that runs,
"If at first you don't succeed, try, try again."
This is nonsense. It ought to read,
"If at first you don't succeed, quit, quit at once."*
STEPHEN LEACOCK

99

Success didn't spoil me;
I've always been insufferable.
FRAN LEBOWITZ

66

Success is that old A B C — ability,
breaks and courage.
CHARLES LUCKMAN

99

The successful people are the ones who
think up things for the rest of the world
to keep busy at.
DON MARQUIS

66

Be nice to people on the way up because you'll
meet 'em on your way down.
WILSON MIZNER

99

Nothing fails like success.
GERALD NACHMAN

66

Failures are like skinned knees . . . painful but
superficial, they heal quickly.
H. ROSS PEROT

99

You always pass failure on the way to success.
MICKEY ROONEY

66

Failure changes for the better,
success for the worse.
SENECA

99

To climb steep hills
Requires slow pace at first.
WILLIAM SHAKESPEARE

66

I never climbed any ladder: I have achieved
eminence by sheer gravitation.
GEORGE BERNARD SHAW

99

The higher a monkey climbs,
the more you see of its behind.
JOSEPH STILWELL

66

Whenever a friend succeeds,
a little something in me dies.
GORE VIDAL

99

*I always turn to the sports pages first, which record
people's accomplishments. The front page has
nothing but man's failures.*
EARL WARREN

66

There is always room at the top.
DANIEL WEBSTER

99

*Don't ever make the same mistake twice —
unless it pays.*
MAE WEST

66

*She's the kind of girl who climbed the ladder of
success wrong by wrong.*
MAE WEST

99

*Experience is the name so many people give to
their mistakes.*
OSCAR WILDE

66

Success is simply a matter of luck. Ask any failure.
EARL WILSON

Success and failure: proverbs

Better poor with honor than rich with shame.

Busiest men find the most leisure time.

Failure brings experience and experience brings wisdom.

He that labors and thrives, spins gold.

He who begins many things finishes few.

I will win the horse or lose the saddle.

If a job's worth doing, it's worth doing well.

If at first you don't succeed, try, try, try again.

If you don't make mistakes you don't make anything.

Man learns little from success, but much from failure.

Misfortune arrives quickly but departs slowly.

Nothing succeeds like success.

Opportunity seldom knocks twice.

Payday comes every day.

*Some men promise more in a day than
they fulfill in a year.*

Sometimes the best gain is to lose.

Success has many friends.

Success makes a fool seem wise.

The more you get, the more you want.

*The vulgar will keep no record of your hits,
only your misses.*

Those who climb high often have a fall.

*Wealth is not his who makes it,
but his who enjoys it.*

*What you lose on the swings
you gain on the roundabouts.*

Television

66

*TV — a clever contraction
derived from the words
Terrible Vaudeville . . . we
call it a medium because
nothing's well done.*
GOODMAN ACE

99

*The human race is faced
with a cruel choice: work
or daytime television.*
ANONYMOUS

66

*Do you realize if it weren't for Edison we'd be
watching TV by candlelight?*
AL BOLISKA

99

*Television is more interesting than people. If it were
not, we would have people standing in the corners
of our rooms.*
ALAN CORENK

66

*Culture . . . television programmes so boring that
they cannot be classified as entertainment.*
QUENTIN CRISP

99

Television enables you to be entertained in your home by people you wouldn't have in your home.
DAVID FROST

66

Why should people pay good money to go out and see bad films when they can stay at home and see bad television for nothing?
SAM GOLDWYN

99

Television has proved that people will look at anything rather than each other.
ANN LANDERS

66

I find television very educating. Every time somebody turns on the set I go into the other room and read a book.
GROUCHO MARX

99

It used to be that we in films were the lowest form of art. Now we have something to look down on.
BILLY WILDER

66

Getting an award from TV is like being kissed by someone with bad breath.
MASON WILLIAMS

Travel

"
The town was so dull that when the tide went out it refused to come back.
FRED ALLEN
"

Air travel will be much safer when they eliminate the automobile ride between the city and the airport.
ANONYMOUS

"
If a man has anything in him travel will bring it out, especially ocean travel.
ANONYMOUS

"
The crow, when traveling abroad, came back just as black.
ANONYMOUS

"
Travel broadens the mind.
ANONYMOUS

99

*Do Not Disturb signs
should be written in the language
of the hotel maids.*
TIM BEDORE

66

*In America there are two classes of travel —
first class and with children.*
ROBERT BENCHLEY

99

*Passport: a document treacherously inflicted
upon a citizen going abroad,
exposing him as an alien and pointing
him out for special reprobation and outrage.*
AMBROSE BIERCE

66

*Airline travel is hours of boredom
interrupted by moments of stark terror.*
AL BOLISKA

99

*I can't say I was ever lost,
but I was bewildered once for three days.*
DANIEL BOONE

66

My first rule of travel is never to go to a place that sounds like a medical condition, and Critz clearly was an incurable disease involving flaking skin.
BILL BRYSON

99

Lovers of air travel find it exhilarating to hang poised between the illusion of immortality and the fact of death.
ALEXANDER CHASE

66

Polar exploration is at once the cleanest and most isolated way of having a bad time which has been devised.
APSLEY CHERRY-GARRARD

99

The only way to be sure of catching a train is to miss the one before it.
G.K. CHESTERTON

66

They say travel broadens the mind; but you must have the mind.
G.K. CHESTERTON

99

When we are young we travel to see the world, afterwards to make sure it is still there.
CYRIL CONNOLLY

66

*Too often travel, instead of broadening the mind,
merely lengthens the conversation.*
ELIZABETH DREW

99

At my age travel broadens the behind.
STEPHEN FRY

66

*The odds against there being a bomb on a plane
are a million to one, and against two bombs a
million times a million to one. Next time you fly, cut
the odds and take a bomb.*
BENNY HILL

99

I like terra firma — the more firma, the less terra.
GEORGE S. KAUFMAN

66

*Natives who beat drums to drive off evil spirits are
objects of scorn to smart American who blow horns
to break up traffic jams.*
MARY ELLEN KELLY

99

*I feel about airplanes the way I feel about diets.
It seems to me that they are wonderful things for
other people to go on.*
JEAN KERR

66

Down to Gehenna or up to the throne,
He travels the fastest who travels alone.
RUDYARD KIPLING

99

If you look like your passport photo, you're too ill
to travel.
WILL KOMMEN

66

Thanks to the Interstate Highway System, it is now
possible to travel from coast to coast without
seeing anything.
CHARLES KURALT

99

A man travels the world over in search of what he
needs and returns home to find it.
GEORGE MOORE

66

Rush hour: that hour when traffic is almost at a
standstill.
J.B. MORTON

99

Giannini and I were adhering to
the two key rules of world travel:
1. Never run out of whiskey.
2. Never run out of whiskey.
P.J. O'ROURKE

66

In an underdeveloped country don't drink the water, in a developed country, don't breathe the air.
JONATHAN RABAN

99

Travel is ninety percent anticipation and ten percent recollection.
EDWARD STREETER

66

A city is like a magnet — the bigger it is, the greater the drawing power.
SAMUEL TENENBAUM

99

Travel is fatal to prejudice, bigotry, and narrow-mindedness.
MARK TWAIN

66

Commuter — One who spends his life in riding to and from his wife; A man who shaves and takes a train, And then rides back to shave again.
E.B. WHITE

99

If you look like your passport photo, in all probability you need the journey.
EARL WILSON

Truth and lies

66

Too much truth is uncouth.
FRANKLIN P. ADAMS

99

*Truth never dies but lives
a wretched life.*
ANONYMOUS

66

It was being economical with the truth.
ROBERT ARMSTRONG

99

*She . . . tells enough white lies to ice a wedding
cake.*
MARGOT ASQUITH

66

Truth: that which is negated by the small print.
GERALD BARZAN

99

*For every time She shouted "Fire!"
They only answered "Little Liar!"
And therefore when her Aunt returned,
Matilda and the House, were Burned.*
HILAIRE BELLOC

❝

A truth that's told with bad intent
Beats all the lies you can invent.
WILLIAM BLAKE

❞

Any fool can tell the truth, but it requires a man of
some sense to know how to lie well.
SAMUEL BUTLER

❝

For things said false and never meant,
Do oft prove true by accident.
SAMUEL BUTLER

❞

Some men love truth so much
that they seem to be in continual fear lest she
should catch a cold on overexposure.
SAMUEL BUTLER

❝

A lie can be half-way round the world before the
truth has got its boots on.
JAMES CALLAGHAN

❞

There are a terrible lot of lies going about
the world, and the worst of it is that
half of them are true.
WINSTON CHURCHILL

"

*Truth for him was a moving target; he never aimed
for the bull and rarely pierced the outer ring.*
HUGH CUDLIPP

"

Better a noble lie than a miserable truth.
ROBERTSON DAVIES

"

*The camera cannot lie.
But it can be an accessory to untruth.*
HAORLD EVANS

"

*Truth is something you stumble into
when you think you're going someplace else.*
JERRY GARCIA

"

An exaggeration is a truth that has lost its temper.
KAHLIL GIBRAN

"

Truth, like a torch, the more it's shook it shines.
WILLIAM HAMILTON

"

*A half truth in argument, like a half brick,
carries better.*
STEPHEN LEACOCK

99

Blurting out the complete truth is considered adorable in the young, right smack up to the moment that the child says, "Mommy, is this the fat lady you can't stand?"
JUDITH MARTIN

66

She's too crafty a woman to invent a new lie when an old one will serve.
W. SOMERSET MAUGHAM

99

It is hard to believe that a man is telling the truth when you know that you would lie if you were in his place.
H.L. MENCKEN

66

A little inaccuracy sometimes saves tons of explanation.
SAKI

99

I never give them hell. I just tell the truth and they think it's hell.
HARRY S. TRUMAN

66

The pure and simple truth is rarely pure and never simple.
OSCAR WILDE

War

66

*An infallible method of
conciliating a tiger is to
allow oneself to be
devoured.*
KONRAD ADENAUER

99

*Join the army, see the
world, meet interesting
people — and kill 'em.*
WOODY ALLEN

66

In time of war the devil makes more room in hell.
ANONYMOUS

99

*It is better to be a coward for a minute than dead
for the rest of your life.*
ANONYMOUS

66

*It is the blood of the soldier
that makes the general great.*
ANONYMOUS

99

War does not determine who is right —
only who is left.
ANONYMOUS

66

Peace might sell, but who's buying?
JOAN BAEZ

99

War would end if the dead could return.
STANLEY BALDWIN

66

The world is a madhouse, so it's only right that it is
patrolled by armed idiots.
BRENDAN BEHAN

99

Battle: a method of untying with the teeth a
political knot that will not yield to the tongue.
AMBROSE BIERCE

66

Peace: in international affairs, a period of cheating
between two periods of fighting.
AMBROSE BIERCE

99

Formerly when great fortunes were only made in war, war was a business; but now when great fortunes are only made by business, business is war.
CHRISTIAN N. BOVEE

66

The way to win an atomic war is to make certain it never starts.
OMAR BRADLEY

99

I beat the army by being declared psychoneurotic. They thought I was crazy. When I filled in their forms, under "Race," I wrote: "Human." Under "Color:" "It varies."
MARLON BRANDO

66

The best defence against the atom bomb is not to be there when it goes off.
THE BRITISH ARMY JOURNAL

99

I was put in the combat engineers. We would throw up bridges in advance of the infantry but mainly we would just throw up.
MEL BROOKS

❝

*People who fight fire with fire
usually end up with ashes.*
ABIGAIL VAN BUREN

❞

*You can get more with a kind word and a gun than
you can with a kind word alone.*
AL CAPONE

❝

*A prisoner of war is a man who tries to kill you and
fails, and then asks you not to kill him.*
WINSTON CHURCHILL

❞

*Being in the army is like being in the Boy Scouts,
except that the Boy Scouts have adult supervision.*
BLAKE CLARK

❝

*Military justice is to justice
what military music is to music.*
GEORGES CLEMENCEAU

❞

*Admirals extolled for standing still,
Or doing nothing with a deal of skill.*
WILLIAM COWPER

❝

*In the final choice a soldier's pack
is not so heavy as a prisoner's chains.*
DWIGHT D. EISENHOWER

❞

*Do not needlessly endanger your lives until I give
you the signal.*
DWIGHT D. EISENHOWER

❝

*I think that people want peace so much that one of
these days government had better get out of their
way and let them have it.*
DWIGHT D. EISENHOWER

❞

*We are going to have peace even if we have to fight
for it.*
DWIGHT D. EISENHOWER

❝

Peace is a continuation of war by other means.
VO NGUYEN GIAP

❞

*When I hear the word "gun" I reach for my
culture.*
I.J. GOOD

66

Deference is our primary mission, and peace is our profession. We have a mixed force of bombers and missiles to carry out this mission.
BRUCE C. HALLOWAY

99

Fortunately, just when things were blackest, the war broke out.
JOSEPH HELLER

66

How is the world ruled and how do wars start? Diplomats tell lies to journalists and then believe what they read.
KARL KRAUS

99

If you don't want to use the army, I should like to borrow it for a while.
ABRAHAM LINCOLN (to George B. McClellan for non-aggressiveness)

66

War is only a cowardly escape from the problems of peace.
THOMAS MANN

99

Military intelligence is a contradiction in terms.
GROUCHO MARX

"

Nothing raises morale better than a dead general.
JOHN MASTERS

"

Fighting is like champagne. It goes to the heads of cowards as quickly as of heroes.
MARGARET MITCHELL

"

Soldiers win battles and generals get the medals.
NAPOLEON BONAPARTE

"

No man can think clearly when his fists are clenched.
GEORGE JEAN NATHAN

"

The quickest way of ending a war is to lose it.
GEORGE ORWELL

"

The object of war is not to die for your country but to make the other bastard die for his.
GEORGE PATTON

"

If sunbeams were weapons of war we would have had solar energy long ago.
GEORGE PORTER

99

One murder makes a villain, millions a hero.
BEILBY PORTEUS

66

*History is littered with wars which everybody knew
would never happen.*
ENOCH POWELL

99

*The Army Selection Board told me I had the voice
of a gentleman and the spelling of a clown. What
spelling had to do with winning wars is beyond me.*
OLIVER REED

66

*Patriotism is the willingness to kill and be killed
for trivial reasons.*
BERTRAND RUSSELL

99

*Politics is war without bloodshed,
and war is politics with blood.*
MAO TSE-TUNG

66

Only the winners decide what were war crimes.
GARY WILLS

Wit and humor

"

Hanging is too good for a man who makes puns; he should be drawn and quoted.
FRED ALLEN

"

Sharp wits, like sharp knives, do often cut their owner's fingers.
ARROWSMITH

"

The marvellous thing about a joke with a double meaning is that it can only mean one thing.
RONNIE BARKER

"

He who laughs has not yet heard the bad news.
BERTOLT BRECHT

"

A man of wit would often be embarrassed without the company of fools.
LA ROCHEFOUCAULD

99

*A pun is the lowest form of humor — when you
don't think of it first.*
OSCAR LEVANT

66

*A person reveals his character by nothing so
clearly as a joke he resents.*
GEORGE CHRISTOPH LICHTENBERG

99

*A satirist is a man who discovers unpleasant things
about himself and then says them about other
people.*
PETER MCARTHUR

66

*All human race would fain be wits,
And millions miss for one that hits.*
JONATHAN SWIFT

99

*Humor plays close to the big, hot fire, which is the
truth, and the reader feels the heat.*
E.B. WHITE

66

*She had a penetrating sort of laugh. Rather like a
train going into a tunnel.*
P.G. WODEHOUSE

Women

66

*Mothers love their sons
more than they love their
husbands — after all, they
created their sons but only
chose their husbands.*
ANONYMOUS

99

*Women can do everything;
men can do the rest.*
ANONYMOUS

66

*Take a close-up of a woman past sixty. You might
as well use a picture of a relief map of Ireland!*
NANCY ASTOR

99

Most women are not so young as they are painted.
MAX BEERBOHM

66

*Woman would be more charming if one could fall
into her arms without falling into her hands.*
AMBROSE BIERCE

66

Brigands demand your money or your life; women require both.
SAMUEL BUTLER

99

Being a woman is a terribly difficult trade, since it consists primarily of dealing with men.
JOSEPH CONRAD

66

One is not born a woman, one becomes one.
SIMONE DE BEAUVOIR

99

There's a difference between beauty and charm. A beautiful woman is one I notice. A charming woman is one who notices me.
JOHN ERSKINE

66

Housework is what woman does that nobody notices unless she hasn't done it.
EVAN ESAR

99

Never try to impress a woman, because if you do she'll expect you to keep up the standard for the rest of your life.
W.C. FIELDS

66

Women are like elephants to me — I like to look at 'em, but I wouldn't want to own one.
W.C. FIELDS

99

You have to admit that most women who have done something with their lives have been disliked by almost everyone.
FRANÇOISE GILOT

66

Women give us solace, but if it were not for women we should never need solace.
DON HEROLD

99

Women have a wonderful sense of right and wrong, but little sense of right and left.
DON HEROLD

66

A woman has to be twice as good as a man to go half as far.
FANNIE HURST

99

Women prefer men who have something tender about them — especially the legal kind.
KAY INGRAM

66

A woman occasionally is quite a serviceable substitute for masturbation. It takes an abundance of imagination, to be sure.
KARL KRAUS

99

The average girl would rather have beauty than brains because she knows that the average man can see much better than he can think.
LADIES' HOME JOURNAL

66

But if God had wanted us to think with our wombs, why did He give us a brain?
CLARE BOOTHE LUCE

99

Anyone who says he can see through women is missing a lot.
GROUCHO MARX

66

She got her good looks from her father. He's a plastic surgeon.
GROUCHO MARX

99

Women should be obscene and not heard.
GROUCHO MARX

66

A woman will always sacrifice herself if you give her the opportunity. It's her favorite form of self-indulgence.
W. SOMERSET MAUGHAM

99

On one issue, at least, men and women agree: they both distrust women.
H.L. MENCKEN

66

The allurement that women hold out to men is precisely the allurement that Cape Hatteras holds out to sailors: they are enormously dangerous and hence enormously fascinating.
H.L. MENCKEN

99

When a woman inclines to learning there is usually something wrong with her sexual apparatus.
FRIEDRICH W. NIETZSCHE

66

Women are like banks. Breaking and entering is a serious business.
JOE ORTON

99

Most hierarchies were established by men who now monopolize the upper levels, thus depriving women of their rightful share of opportunities to achieve incompetence.
LAURENCE J. PETER

66

There's nothing so similar to one poodle dog as another poodle dog, and that goes for women, too.
PABLO PICASSO

99

The charms of a passing woman are usually in direct relation to the speed of her passing.
MARCEL PROUST

66

Woman is like a teabag — you can't tell how strong she is until you put her in hot water.
NANCY REAGAN

99

The only problem with women is men.
KATHIE SARACHILD

"

*The one point on which all women are in furious
secret rebellion against the existing law is the
saddling of the right to a child with the obligation
to become the servant of a man.*
GEORGE BERNARD SHAW

"

*Once made equal to man, woman
becomes his superior.*
SOCRATES

"

*Social science affirms that a woman's place in
society marks the level of civilization.*
ELIZABETH CADY STANTON

"

A woman reading Playboy *feels a little like
a Jew reading a Nazi manual.*
GLORIA STEINEM

"

*A woman without a man is like a
fish without a bicycle.*
GLORIA STEINEM

"

We are becoming the men we wanted to marry.
GLORIA STEINEM

66

*It is clearly absurd that it should be possible
for a woman to qualify as a saint . . . while
she may not qualify as a curate.*
MARY STOCKS

99

*I hate women because they always
know where things are.*
JAMES THURBER

66

*Women with "pasts" interest men because men
hope that history will repeat itself.*
MAE WEST

99

*My advice to the women's clubs of America is to
raise more hell and fewer dahlias.*
WILLIAM ALLEN WHITE

66

*Whatever women do they must do twice as
well as men to be thought half as good. Luckily
this is not difficult.*
CHARLOTTE WHITTON

99

*A woman will flirt with anybody in the world as
long as other people are looking on.*
OSCAR WILDE

Women: proverbs

A bad woman is worse than a bad man.

A poor beauty finds more lovers than husbands.

A sieve will hold water better than a woman's mouth a secret.

A woman without virtue is like a tasteless wine.

A woman who accepts, sells herself; a woman who gives, surrenders.

A woman's in pain, a woman's in woe, a woman is ill when she likes to be so.

A woman's sword is her tongue, and she does not let it rust.

A woman's thoughts are afterthoughts.

Beauty and honesty seldom agree.

Between a woman's "yes" and "no" there is no room for the point of a needle.

Beware of a bad woman, and put no trust in a good one.

Fortune is a woman; if you neglect her today, expect not to regain her tomorrow.

No woman is ugly if she is well dressed.

She who is born a beauty is born betrothed.

Trust not a woman when she weeps.

Women are as fickle as April weather.

Women are like wasps in their anger.

Women are necessary evils.

Women are saints in church, angels in the street, and devils at home.

Women in state affairs are like monkeys in glass shops.

Women laugh when they can, and weep when they will.

Work

66

*All work and no play
makes Jack a dull boy.*
ANONYMOUS

99

*Because the first day back
at work hurts so much, I
find it better to start work
on the second.*
ANONYMOUS

66

No bees, no honey; no work, no money.
ANONYMOUS

99

*The difference between an amateur and a
professional is an amateur gives up when
encountering difficulties and a professional
speeds up.*
ANONYMOUS

66

*We are the unwilling, led by the unqualified, doing
the unnecessary for the ungrateful.*
ANONYMOUS

99

When in charge, meditate. When in doubt, mumble.
When in difficulty, delegate.
ANONYMOUS

66

When the going gets tough, the tough get going.
ANONYMOUS

99

Being in your own business is working eighty hours
a week so that you can avoid working forty hours a
week for someone else.
RAMONA E.F. ARNETT

66

Nothing is really work unless you would rather be
doing something else.
J.M. BARRIE

99

Choose a job that you like, and you will not have to
work a day of your life.
CONFUCIUS

66

Absence of occupation is not rest,
A mind quite vacant is a mind distress'd.
WILLIAM COWPER

99

It is better to wear out than to rust out.
RICHARD CUMBERLAND

66

I don't work — I live.
GÉRARD DEPARDIEU

99

Nothing demonstrates authority better than silence.
CHARLES DE GAULLE

66

*I never did anything worth doing by accident, nor
did any of my inventions come by accident; they
came by work.*
THOMAS EDISON

99

There is no substitute for hard work.
THOMAS EDISON

66

He who shuns the millstone, shuns the meal.
ERASMUS

99

*All work and no play makes Jack a dull boy —
and Jill a wealthy widow.*
EVAN ESAR

66

We always admire the other fellow more after we have tried his job.
WILLIAM FEATHER

99

Life is work, and everything you undertake adds to your experience.
HENRY FORD

66

I have long been of the opinion that if work were such a splendid thing the rich would have kept more of it for themselves.
BRUCE GROCOTT

99

God gives every bird its food, but he does not throw it into the nest.
J.G. HOLLAND

66

I'm a great believer in luck, and I find the harder I work the more I have of it.
THOMAS JEFFERSON

99

It is impossible to enjoy idling thoroughly unless one has plenty of work to do.
JEROME K. JEROME

❝

Most people like hard work. Particularly when they are paying for it.
FRANKLIN P. JONES

❞

A farm is a hunk of land on which, if you get up early enough mornings and work late enough nights, you'll make a fortune —
if you strike oil on it.
JIM JORDAN

❝

When your work speaks for itself, don't interrupt.
HENRY J. KAISER

❞

All jobs should be open to everybody, unless they actually require a penis or a vagina.
FLORYNCE KENNEDY

❝

The desire to work is so rare that it must be encouraged wherever it is found.
ABRAHAM LINCOLN

❞

When a man tells you he got rich through hard work, ask him "Whose?"
DON MARQUIS

66

Life is too short to do anything for oneself that one can pay others to do for one.
W. SOMERSET MAUGHAM

99

If you don't want to work you have to work to earn enough money so that you won't have to work.
OGDEN NASH

66

People who work sitting down get paid more than people who work standing up.
OGDEN NASH

99

Work expands so as to fill the time available for its completion.
NORTHCOTE PARKINSON

66

They say hard work never hurt anybody, but I figure why take the chance.
RONALD REAGAN

99

One of the greatest labor-saving inventions of today is tomorrow.
VINCENT T. ROSS

66

Work is of two kinds: first, altering the position of matter at or near the earth's surface relative to other matter; second, telling other people to do so.
BERTRAND RUSSELL

99

The only place where success comes before work is a dictionary.
VIDAL SASSOON

66

I'm a classic example of all humorists — only funny when I'm working.
PETER SELLERS

99

Fie upon this quiet life, I want work.
WILLIAM SHAKESPEARE

66

Wherever a man works, he leaves something of his soul.
HENRYK SIENKIEWICZ

99

The test of a vocation is the love of the drudgery it involves.
LOGAN PEARSALL SMITH

66

People who work a lot do not work hard.
HENRY DAVID THOREAU

99

*Early to rise and early to bed makes a male
healthy and wealthy and dead.*
JAMES THURBER

66

*The trouble with the rat race is that even if
you win, you're still a rat.*
LILY TOMLIN

99

*It's not how many hours you put in, it's what you
get done while you're working.*
DONALD TRUMP

66

*Work is the refuge of people who have
nothing better to do.*
OSCAR WILDE

99

*It was not as difficult as it seemed. Actually, all I
had to do was work nonstop.*
ROBERT WOODRUFF

Writers

66

*Why spoil a good story
for want of some
plausible facts.*
ANONYMOUS

99

*It took me fifteen years to
discover I had no talent for
writing, but I couldn't give
it up because by that time
I was too famous.*
ROBERT BENCHLEY

66

*I've always believed in writing without a
collaborator, because where two people are writing
the same book, each believes he gets all the worries
and only half the royalties.*
AGATHA CHRISTIE

99

*A good storyteller is a person who has a good memory
and hopes other people haven't.*
IRWIN S. COBB

66

*In America only the successful writer is important,
in France all writers are important, in England
no writer is important, and in Australia you have
to explain what a writer is.*
GEOFFREY COTTRELL

99

*An autobiography is an obituary in serial form
with the last installment missing.*
QUENTIN CRISP

66

*The author who speaks about his own books is almost
as bad as a mother who talks about her own children.*
BENJAMIN DISRAELI

99

*What an author likes to write most is his signature
on the back of a check.*
BRENDAN FRANCIS

66

*Next to the writer of real estate advertisements, the
autobiographer is the most suspect of prose artists.*
DONAL HENAHAN

99

No man but a blockhead ever wrote except for money.
SAMUEL JOHNSON

66

*One man is as good as another until he
has written a book.*
BENJAMIN JOWETT

99

*When once the itch of literature comes over a man,
nothing can cure it but the scratching of a pen.*
SAMUEL LOVER

66

*A person who publishes a book appears willfully in
public with his pants down.*
EDNA ST. VINCENT MILLAY

99

*Writing is the hardest way of earning a living, with the
possible exception of wrestling alligators.*
OLIN MILLER

66

*I wrote a short story because I wanted to see something
of mine in print other than my fingers.*
WILSON MIZNER

99

*If you steal from one author, it's plagiarism;
if you steal from many, it's research.*
WILSON MIZNER

❝

*A pin has as much head as some authors,
and a good deal more point.*
GEORGE D. PRENTICE

❞

*My problem is that I am not frightfully interested in
anything, except myself. And of all forms of fiction
autobiography is the most gratuitous.*
TOM STOPPARD

❝

*A writer judging his own work is like a deceived
husband — he is frequently the last person to
appreciate the true state of affairs.*
ROBERT TRAVER

❞

*I never can understand how two men can write
a book together; to me that's like three people
getting together to have a baby.*
EVELYN WAUGH

❝

*A writer is like a bean plant — he has his little
day, and then gets stringy.*
E.B. WHITE

Author index

If you liked this book, you'll love all the titles in this series: